S. Hrg. 113–179

A DANGEROUS SLIDE BACKWARDS: RUSSIA'S DETERIORATING HUMAN RIGHTS

JOINT HEARING

BEFORE THE

SUBCOMMITTEE ON INTERNATIONAL OPERATIONS AND ORGANIZATIONS, HUMAN RIGHTS, DEMOCRACY, AND GLOBAL WOMEN'S ISSUES

AND THE

SUBCOMMITTEE ON EUROPEAN AFFAIRS

OF THE

COMMITTEE ON FOREIGN RELATIONS UNITED STATES SENATE

ONE HUNDRED THIRTEENTH CONGRESS

FIRST SESSION

JUNE 13, 2013

Printed for the use of the Committee on Foreign Relations

Available via the World Wide Web: http://www.gpo.gov/fdsys/

U.S. GOVERNMENT PRINTING OFFICE

86–776 PDF   WASHINGTON : 2014

For sale by the Superintendent of Documents, U.S. Government Printing Office
Internet: bookstore.gpo.gov   Phone: toll free (866) 512–1800; DC area (202) 512–1800
Fax: (202) 512–2104   Mail: Stop IDCC, Washington, DC 20402–0001

COMMITTEE ON FOREIGN RELATIONS

ROBERT MENENDEZ, New Jersey, *Chairman*

BARBARA BOXER, California
BENJAMIN L. CARDIN, Maryland
ROBERT P. CASEY, JR., Pennsylvania
JEANNE SHAHEEN, New Hampshire
CHRISTOPHER A. COONS, Delaware
RICHARD J. DURBIN, Illinois
TOM UDALL, New Mexico
CHRISTOPHER MURPHY, Connecticut
TIM KAINE, Virginia

BOB CORKER, Tennessee
JAMES E. RISCH, Idaho
MARCO RUBIO, Florida
RON JOHNSON, Wisconsin
JEFF FLAKE, Arizona
JOHN McCAIN, Arizona
JOHN BARRASSO, Wyoming
RAND PAUL, Kentucky

DANIEL E. O'BRIEN, *Staff Director*
LESTER E. MUNSON III, *Republican Staff Director*

SUBCOMMITTEE ON INTERNATIONAL OPERATIONS AND ORGANIZATIONS, HUMAN RIGHTS, DEMOCRACY, AND GLOBAL WOMEN'S ISSUES

BARBARA BOXER, California, *Chairman*

ROBERT P. CASEY, JR., PENNSYLVANIA
JEANNE SHAHEEN, New Hampshire
RICHARD J. DURBIN, Illinois
TIM KAINE, Virginia

RAND PAUL, Kentucky
JAMES E. RISCH, Idaho
MARCO RUBIO, Florida
RON JOHNSON, Wisconsin

SUBCOMMITTEE ON EUROPEAN AFFAIRS

CHRISTOPHER MURPHY, Connecticut, *Chairman*

ROBERT P. CASEY, JR., Pennsylvania
JEANNE SHAHEEN, New Hampshire
CHRISTOPHER A. COONS, Delaware
RICHARD J. DURBIN, Illinois

RON JOHNSON, Wisconsin
JAMES E. RISCH, Idaho
JEFF FLAKE, Arizona
JOHN BARRASSO, Wyoming

CONTENTS

(III)

A DANGEROUS SLIDE BACKWARDS: RUSSIA'S DETERIORATING HUMAN RIGHTS SITUATION

THURSDAY, JUNE 13, 2013

U.S. SENATE, SUBCOMMITTEE ON INTERNATIONAL OPERATIONS AND ORGANIZATIONS, HUMAN RIGHTS, DEMOCRACY, AND GLOBAL WOMEN'S ISSUES AND SUBCOMMITTEE ON EUROPEAN AFFAIRS, COMMITTEE ON FOREIGN RELATIONS,

Washington, DC.

The subcommittees met, pursuant to notice, at 10:26 a.m., in room SD–419, Dirksen Senate Office Building, Hon. Barbara Boxer and Hon. Christopher Murphy (chairmen of the respective subcommittees) presiding.

Present: Senators Boxer, Murphy, Paul, and Johnson.

Also Present: Senator McCain.

OPENING STATEMENT OF HON. BARBARA BOXER, U.S. SENATOR FROM CALIFORNIA

Senator BOXER. Good morning, everybody, and welcome. We apologize for starting late. We had a vote, which happens around here. We are hoping we will have a little bit of a breather, here, so we can hear from all of you before we have to run off again. But, thank you for your patience.

I want to welcome everyone to today's hearing on the deteriorating human rights situation in Russia. This is a joint hearing of the Subcommittee on International Operations and Organizations, Human Rights, and Democracy, and Global Women's Issues and the Subcommittee on European Affairs.

In particular, I wanted to thank Senator Murphy for really working on this very closely with me, and our ranking members, Senators Paul and Johnson, and very happy to see Senator Johnson here with us.

I want to extend a warm welcome to all of our distinguished witnesses.

We are here today to examine the current state of human rights in Russia and to better understand what is taking place within that country today. Let me be clear, I want to see a strong and productive United States relationship with Russia. Russia's been an important partner on a range of issues, from Iran sanctions to Afghanistan to reducing the number of nuclear weapons in the world, and will continue to play a strong and influential role on the global stage.

But, Russia's partnership on a number of issues does not preclude us from taking a hard look at what appears to be a systematic crackdown on internationally recognized basic freedoms, including freedom of association, expression, since President Putin assumed the Presidency for a third time, last year.

Sadly, it appears that no one is immune. President Putin has targeted both Russian NGOs and highly respected international NGOs, including Amnesty International, Human Rights Watch, and Transparency International. He has made it profoundly difficult for any political opposition to organize or to have their voices heard. Most recently, he has targeted public health and environmental advocacy organizations and groups working for the protection of LGBT individuals. He has even put musicians in jail.

And I want to place in the record a statement from several of these musicians, and just read from the last paragraph, ''We urge the United States to take notice of what is happening in Russia, of how we're slipping backwards, not towards progress, but toward repression. We ask you, members of the Senate, to work for the release of our friends, who aren't hooligans or criminals, but women who have strong views and the courage to voice them. Thank you.'' That is a quote, and I would ask unanimous consent if I could put this whole statement into the record. At this time, I will do that.

[EDITOR'S NOTE.—The statement mentioned above can be found in the ''Additional Material Submitted for the Record'' section at the end of this hearing.]

Senator BOXER. In short, it appears that President Putin has little tolerance for anyone who appears to disagree in any way with the policies of his administration. This is a most sad development, particularly for those of us who were encouraged by the opening up of political space in Russia, and we are curious about whether there are any opportunities to help reverse this troublesome tide. And that is what we hope to explore today.

Our first witness is Mr. Frank Jannuzi. Mr. Jannuzi spent over 15 years advising the Senate Foreign Relations Committee as a policy director and working with then-Chairman Kerry on a broad range of issues. He comes to us now as the deputy executive director of Amnesty International USA and the head of the Washington, DC, office.

And then we will hear from Dr. Leon Aron. Dr. Aron was born in Moscow. He came to the United States as a refugee, in June— from Russia, from the Soviet Union—in June 1978, at the age of 24. He is resident scholar and director of Russian studies at the American Enterprise Institute. The author of 3 books and over 300 scholarly articles and essays, Dr. Aron is an expert on matters concerning Russia.

And then we are pleased to have the former U.S. Ambassador at Large for the former Soviet Union, Stephen Sestanovich. In this role, Ambassador Sestanovich was the State Department's principal officer responsible for policy toward Russia and other states of the former Soviet Union from 1997 to 2001. Currently, he is the George F. Kennan senior fellow for Russian and Eurasian Studies at the Council on Foreign Relations and a professor of international diplomacy at Columbia University.

Our fourth witness is Dr. Ariel Cohen, a senior research fellow for Russian and Eurasian studies and international energy policy at the Heritage Foundation. A leading expert on Russia, Eurasia, Eastern Europe, and the Middle East, Dr. Cohen has authored numerous books and has written many articles on Russian, foreign, and domestic policy.

And finally, it is certainly our great pleasure to have the Honorable Boris—oh, I have to say it right—Nemtsov. In addition to being a former Deputy Prime Minister of Russia, Mr. Nemtsov is cochairman of the Republican Party of Russia—People's Freedom Party. In January 2011, he was sentenced to 15 days in jail after taking part in a New Year's Eve opposition rally.

We are grateful for the wealth of knowledge and breadth of experience that our panel members will offer to share with us today.

And I now turn to Senator Johnson, then Senator Murphy, then Senator Paul, for their opening statements.

OPENING STATEMENT OF HON. RON JOHNSON, U.S. SENATOR FROM WISCONSIN

Senator JOHNSON. Thank you, Madam Chair. And I want to thank all the witnesses for appearing here.

In February 2009, Vice President Biden said it was "time to press the reset button with Russia." Secretary Clinton and the administration went out of their way to repair the United States-Russian relationship, some would say at the expense of our European allies. For example, the United States agreed to an unnecessary nuclear arms reduction treaty with Russia which is weighted heavily in Russia's favor. President Obama even offered President Medvedev more flexibility on U.S. missile defense in Europe after his election. It appears that the President has fulfilled that promise.

Despite these accommodations, relations between our two nations have continued to deteriorate. Just this week, in an effort to gain favor with other anti-American leaders, the President proactively offered to considering an asylum request for the American who leaked NSA programs to the press, but no requests have been received for asylum.

Just to name a few issues that we have had with Russia in recent years is Russia's assistance to Iran's nuclear programs and watering down Iran's sanctions of the United States—or, the U.N. Security Council, individual Russian entities providing assistance to Iran's ballistic missile programs, the Russian invasion and continued occupation of Georgia, Russia's war games simulating a nuclear attack on our NATO ally, Poland, and energy disputes with its neighbors, and arms to the Syrian regime, the most recent and probably most damaging example.

Russia could be an extraordinary force for good in the world, but I am troubled by the direction it is turning. It is time to reexamine our policies and learn from our mistakes. Given the current internal situation and the relationship between our governments, it would be hard for anyone to argue that our strategy is working. Americans are truly concerned with the decline of basic fundamental freedoms in Russia. Freedoms of speech and assembly, free and fair elections, and the rule of law are all under assault. The level of corruption makes it hard for businesses to operate.

One of the most troubling issues is the treatment of civil society. Instead of moving toward a more democratic and prosperous nation, the government is backsliding, becoming more authoritarian, corrupt, and hostile to its neighbors.

Today, we have a panel of experts to help Congress as we examine these issues.

Thank you all for being here today. I look forward to learning more about Russia's deteriorating human rights situation and ways in which the U.S. Congress and the administration can work together to adapt our strategy in order to make a difference.

Thank you.

Senator BOXER. Thank you.

Senator Murphy.

OPENING STATEMENT OF HON. CHRISTOPHER MURPHY, U.S. SENATOR FROM CONNECTICUT

Senator MURPHY. Well, thank you very much, Senator Boxer.

And thank you, to your subcommittee, for joining our Subcommittee on European Affairs in this very important hearing.

Thanks to our witnesses for being here, and we want to get to your testimony.

You know, in the 1930s, Josef Stalin carried out a sweeping campaign of political repression in order to consolidate his power—locked up hundreds of thousands of political opponents across Russia. It was called "The Great Purge." What we are witnessing today in Russia, as President Putin cracks down on political dissent and shutters much of civil society, is not yet "The Great Purge," but this hearing will draw light on the dangerous trendlines in Russia that are beginning to suggest that this great nation is backsliding to a part of its history that it should not and cannot repeat.

The question of civil society's role in Russia matters to us because, as Senator Boxer has said, Russia matters to us. It is one of the world's top energy producers, it has got a U.N. Security Council veto, it is a—got a stockpile of 10,000 nuclear warheads in—strategically located at the crossroads of Europe and Asia. More than 1,000 American companies do business in Russia, and Russia is a growing market for American goods and services. The European Union, our largest trading partner, relies on Russia for one-third of its oil and gas imports. We need Russia to be an ally, but it cannot be if the government is constantly continuing this pattern of scaring off or locking up political opponents.

One particularly egregious example of the Russian Government's overreach has been its recent treatment of NGOs. In July of last year, Russia approved a law requiring NGOs that receive any foreign funds, no matter how small the amount, to register as a, "foreign agent." Any NGO that fails to comply would be fined thousands of dollars. And, in addition to limiting NGOs' activities, in a practical manner, the laws have an enormous chilling effect by signaling that groups will be subject to extra scrutiny by the government.

Now, Americans do not provide financial assistance to civil society groups, either individually or collectively through government, in order to undermine other democracies. We do it because we want to help strengthen them. We do it because we want to help empower people to shape their communities, engage with their governments, and ultimately leave their children a better place to live. I strongly hope that the Russian Government will reconsider its approach and allow organizations to operate transparently and receive support in accordance with international norms.

Russia is not yet holding another "Great Purge," but, as the trumped-up arrests mount of the government's political opponents, it is interesting to note that, during "The Great Purge," a Russian brought to court on political charges actually was 20 times more likely to be exonerated than he is today under similar charges. For Russia to be a full-fledged card-carrying member of the international community, this cannot continue.

And I look forward to today's hearing.

Senator BOXER. Thank you, Senator.

Senator Paul.

OPENING STATEMENT OF HON. RAND PAUL, U.S. SENATOR FROM KENTUCKY

Senator PAUL. I want to thank the Chairwoman for convening this hearing on human rights in Russia, and I look forward to hearing from the experts.

Thank you.

Senator BOXER. Thank you very much.

So, we are going to start off with our first witness, Mr. Frank Jannuzi, deputy executive director of Amnesty International.

STATEMENT OF FRANK JANNUZI, DEPUTY EXECUTIVE DIRECTOR OF ADVOCACY, POLICY AND RESEARCH, INTERIM COEXECUTIVE DIRECTOR, AMNESTY INTERNATIONAL, NEW YORK, NY

Mr. JANNUZI. Thank you, Madam Chairwoman. Thank you, members of the panel. It is my honor to appear before you this morning on this side of the table. It feels a little different than being on the other side of the table, but I am very pleased to be here.

As all of the members of this panel have pointed out, freedom is under assault in Russia. New bills passed just this week restrict nongovernmental organizations, criminalize actions that are committed, "to insult religious feelings of believers," and they outlaw activism by lesbian, gay, transsexual individuals, and their supporters. These new laws are coming at a time when political expression, freedom of assembly, freedom of speech in Russia are already deeply constrained.

Amnesty International has developed a timeline infographic that tracks the major clampdown on freedom of expression in Russia. And this infographic tool visually illustrates that arrests and other measures to stifle public dissent are widespread and systematic, and that they have accelerated greatly since Putin's inauguration in 2012.

The clampdown coming as Russia prepares to host the 2014 Sochi Winter Olympics should be a matter of grave concern to all Americans. Moscow's lack of respect for basic human rights speaks volumes about its reliability as an international partner on vital national security issues, whether those are in Syria or nuclear non-proliferation concerns on the Korean Peninsula.

It is not just individuals who are under assault. As Chairwoman Boxer has already said, nongovernmental organizations are coming under enormous scrutiny, labeled as foreign agents, and we are concerned that this is just ''round one.'' Not every organization has the kind of international support and strength that Amnesty International enjoys. We are not worried about our operations in Russia. We are very worried about the more vulnerable groups, especially in Russian civil society.

Let me underscore two important points. The first is that this crackdown is not about silencing opponents only on the political fringes. This is about stifling all who would question consolidation of power under President Putin and his Siloviki allies. President Putin's network is consolidating the power over, not only economic matters, but also political matters. And the influence of his KGB-trained operatives, and their willingness to use force to maintain their status, should not be underestimated.

The second point is that this repression is arguably more pronounced in certain regions of Russia, especially the North Caucasus, where authorities use the excuse of counterterrorism operations to justify all manner of serious human rights violations, from disappearances, torture, or even extrajudicial killings.

I want to try to put a human face on this problem. That is what Amnesty International is known for. Russia's most famous prisoners of conscience at the moment are the members of the band Pussy Riot. Now, inside Russia, and here in Washington, they can be a polarizing group. I am more of a Sondheim fan than I am of their music. But, we should all agree that their brief performance in Christ the Savior Cathedral should not be the cause of years of imprisonment. Amnesty International has developed a viewer guide to accompany the just-released HBO documentary about the band. It is called ''Pussy Riot of Punk Prayer.'' And our viewer guide illustrates how the band members were singled out for their political protest against Putin, and how they were systematically denied a fair trial. We are calling on the Russian authorities to immediately release the two imprisoned band members, Marie Alekhina and Nadya Tolokonnikova.

A quick word about Nadya. I was pleased to host her and her daughter, Ghera, in Washington, DC, last fall. Her daughter, Ghera, is 5 years old. She just wants her mother back. This is the face of the repression in Putin's Russia. It is 5-year-olds taken from their mothers because of 1-minute rock performances.

I know time is short at this hearing, and so let me summarize by going to what I believe you can do.

First, continue to shine a spotlight on what is happening in Russia. To paraphrase the motto of Las Vegas, ''What happens in Moscow must not stay in Moscow.''

Second, insist that President Obama does not give President Putin a get-out-of-the-doghouse-free card when he travels to Russia in September. There should be no reset button on political repression.

Third, join Amnesty International's Defenders of Freedom Program. This is a cooperative joint venture we launched with the

Tom Lantos Human Rights Commission last fall. Every Member of Congress is invited to adopt an amnesty prisoner of conscience. Your voices can unlock cell doors.

And finally, as Senator Murphy has said, find ways to support Russia's budding civil society sector. This is not about turning Russia's civil society activists into foreign agents. It is about recognizing them as foreign partners striving for human rights, rule of law, environmental protection, and other laudable goals.

These steps can make a difference.

I look forward to your questions and thank you for your attention.

[The prepared statement of Mr. Jannuzi follows:]

PREPARED STATEMENT OF FRANK S. JANNUZI

Thanks for inviting me to testify before the Senate Foreign Relations Committee on the subject of Russia's deteriorating human rights situation. I have submitted my full testimony for the record, and request permission to briefly summarize my remarks.

OVERVIEW

In recent months, Russian authorities have intensified their assault on basic freedoms and undermined rule of law. The assault takes many forms. New bills—passed just this week by the country's lower House of Parliament and expected to be approved in the near future by the upper House of Parliament and signed into law by President Vladimir Putin—restrict the activities of nongovernmental organizations, criminalize public actions ''committed to insult the religious feelings of believers'' and outlaw activism by lesbian, gay, bisexual, transgender, and intersex (LGBTI) individuals and their supporters. I would note that the new law criminalizing ''propaganda of nontraditional sexual relations,'' passed 436—by the rubber stamp Duma this week, comes as much of the world marks Pride month.

New controls over the media are being used to smear government critics and bolster the government's policy line. Authorities use secret detention facilities and torture, especially in the North Caucuses region, to silence critics and deny them access to counsel. These measures are widespread and systematic. They are being imposed on domestic and international civil society groups alike.

This crackdown, coming as Russia prepares to host the 2014 Winter Olympics in Sochi, should be a matter of grave concern to the U.S. Government. Moscow's lack of respect for human rights speaks volumes about its reliability as a potential partner to the United States and Europe in addressing pressing international security concerns, from the conflict in Syria to the danger of nuclear proliferation. Moreover, it marks an ominous turn in a country that had been making progress toward developing more open, transparent, and accountable governance.

Many of you may be aware that Amnesty International has itself been subjected to various forms of harassment. For some NGOs, the significance of this particular brand of harassment is that it can result in self-censorship, restriction of activities, or flight. John Dalhuisen, Amnesty International's Europe and Central Asia Director, has expressed our concern that Russia's new NGO law will be used to target prominent civil society organizations. Already 43 Russian nongovernmental organizations in 16 regions are undergoing inspections and investigations, with devastating effect. Many prominent organizations, such as Golos (Voice) Association which monitors elections, the Levada Center for sociological research, the Moscow School for Political Research, and the Human Rights Center Memorial, have been labelled by prosecutors as ''Foreign Agents.'' Our biggest concern is that this is just ''round one,'' and that forced closures are likely to follow.

Indeed, the National Democratic Institute and the International Republican Institute—arms of the National Endowment for Democracy funded by Congress—have already suspended operations in Russia given the threat that their employees might be charged with treason or espionage. This is because the NGO law passed late last year provides for sentences of up to 20 years for individuals ''providing consultative assistance to a foreign organization'' if that group was involved in ''activities aimed against Russia's security,'' a catch-all phrase that could be used to criminalize almost any activity the government deems hostile.

PRISONERS OF CONSCIENCE

Amnesty International coined the term ''Prisoner of Conscience'' to describe individuals who have been imprisoned for the peaceful expression of their beliefs or identity. These individual cases are often emblematic of systemic problems, so let me briefly highlight some cases to underscore two key points:

(1) First, Russia's crackdown is not just about silencing opponents at the political fringes. It is about stifling all who would question the consolidation of power under President Putin and his Federal Security Service (FSB) siloviki associates. This network of former and current state security officers is consolidating control over all key political and economic levers of power in Russia. The influence of these KGB-trained operatives, and their willingness to use force to maintain their privileged status, should not be underestimated.

(2) Second, while the stifling of dissent is widespread, it is arguably most pronounced in the North Caucuses region, home to violent insurrections against Russian rule for centuries. Human rights defenders who bravely speak out about the situation in the North Caucuses region are particularly at risk.

Russia's most famous Prisoners of Conscience are the members of the band Pussy Riot. Pussy Riot's 1-minute long performance in Christ the Savior Cathedral in Moscow, and the band members' subsequent arrest and sentencing, sparked a global outcry and brought Russia's mounting repression to an international audience. The YouTube video of their punk performance, in which they criticized President Putin, generated over 3,000,000 YouTube views.

Amnesty International championed the case of Pussy Riot, not because we have an opinion on their musicality—I am more of a Sondheim fan myself—but because we recognize that artists are often at the cutting edge of political commentary. When artists are arrested for exercising their fundamental right to freedom of expression—whether in China with painter and sculptor Ai Wei Wei, in Egypt with TV Bassem Youssef, or in Burma with comic Zarganar—broader restrictions on the general public are likely to follow.

Two of three Pussy Riot members remain imprisoned, and Amnesty International has designated them as Prisoners of Conscience. We are calling on Russian authorities to immediately and unconditionally release Maria Alekhina and Nadezhda Tolokonnikova and clear all charges against them.

Nadezhda ''Nadya'' Tolokonnikova is serving a 2- year sentence at the notoriously brutal IK–14 women's penal colony in the Republic of Mordovia. Prior to her arrest, Nadya was a student of philosophy at Moscow State University and split her time juggling the demands of being a student, mother, and a political activist. Her daughter Ghera is 5 years old. I had the honor to meet Ghera last fall when I hosted her along with a more famous human rights activist—Daw Aung San Suu Kyi—at the Newseum. Ghera misses her mommy very much.

The second jailed Pussy Riot band member, also a Prisoner of Conscience, is Maria "Masha" Alekhina. Masha has a 4-year-old son, Philip. She was a senior at the Institute of Journalism and Creative Writing in Moscow prior to her arrest. Masha is serving the rest of her term in Perm Krai, a Siberian region notorious for hosting some of the Soviet Union's harshest gulags. Like Ghera, Masha's son misses his mother very much.

An HBO documentary—"Pussy Riot: A Punk Prayer"—debuted this week, and Amnesty International, in collaboration with the producers, has produced a viewing guide, available at our Web site www.amnestyusa.org. Concerned citizens—including Members of Congress—can also express solidarity for the band members by visiting pussyriot.amnestyusa.org.

Unfortunately, the case of Pussy Riot is just the tip of the iceberg when it comes to political repression in Putin's Russia. Other critics of the government—less colorful, perhaps, but no less brave—suffer in obscurity. They are likely to be treated even more harshly than their more famous kindred spirits.

The situation is especially grave in the North Caucasus region, which has been characterized by insecurity and armed attacks on security forces, civilians, and local officials. Many Americans may have first become aware of this region during the Boston Marathon bombing, but the region has long been troubled. Heavy-handed security operations have led to human rights violations such as extrajudicial executions, enforced disappearances, secret detention, torture, and other forms of ill-treatment.

The absence of rule of law fuels unrest. The criminal justice system of Russia is set up to deliver quick convictions, not justice. Defense lawyers are often seen as obstacles to law enforcement officers, who would prefer to see them removed from the equation altogether. Lawyers who dare to defend individuals suspected of membership in armed groups are themselves often threatened, attacked, or murdered by law enforcement officials. Complaints against law enforcement officials often receive no response, are dismissed, or are countered by criminal investigations against those who have filed the complaint.

The case of Sapiyat Magomedova is emblematic. As a defense lawyer, Magomedova is known for her work on cases involving human rights violations committed by law enforcement agencies in Dagestan. In June 2010, when she went to the Khasavyurt town police station to visit a client, police officers prevented her from gaining access to her client. They forcibly removed her from the police station and physically assaulted her. When she attempted to file a complaint about the attack, the police launched their own investigation saying that she in fact attacked them. Investigators repeatedly tried to pressure her into withdrawing her complaint, and warned her that she would face criminal charges herself if she pressed ahead. She refused to be intimidated. In the end, the courts dismissed both complaints—hers and that of the police—without explanation. While some might have interpreted this as a victory, she doesn't see it that way, and neither does Amnesty International. When police assault lawyers simply for attempting to do their jobs, the authorities should hold those police accountable. Magomedova is still seeking justice, and still being persecuted for her persistence. Just last month, Magomedova reported receiving death threats via text messages. Amnesty International stands beside this brave human rights defender and supports her call for justice and accountability.

WHAT CAN BE DONE?

There are no quick fixes to reverse the ever shrinking space for freedom of expression in Russia. A blend of public and private initiatives may work best. Let me suggest four things the members of this committee can do to perhaps deter some of the worst of the abuses and support those inside Russia who are courageously doing their part to advance human rights and rule of law.

- First, continue to shine a spotlight on what is happening and help the American people understand why they should care. Ideally, you should synchronize your efforts with parliamentarians in Europe and through the Helsinki process, because when you speak in unison with your fellow legislators, your voices are amplified. Russia is a great power with enormous potential to help solve the world's problems. But what happens in Moscow does NOT stay in Moscow. It speaks volumes about Russia's reliability as a global partner of the United States in every field, from trade to international security.
- Second, insist that when President Obama travels to Russia in September, that he put human rights prominently on his summit agenda. The Russian Government cares about its reputation, and the United States should not give President Putin a free pass on repression.
- Third, join Amnesty International's Defenders of Freedom program, a cooperative venture we launched last fall with the Tom Lantos Human Rights Commission and the International Religious Freedom Commission. You can adopt a certified Amnesty Prisoner of Conscience and tell their story on your web pages, give floor statements about them, and pass resolutions calling for their release. YOUR voices can help unlock cell doors, and we've already done the research work for you.
- Finally, notwithstanding budget pressures and Russian restrictions, you can generously support funding for nongovernmental organizations striving to strengthen Russian civil society. Training in international human rights law for journalists, lawyers, judges, and even public security officials can improve their performance and better equip them to be human rights champions. And let me say for the record that this is NOT an appeal for funding for Amnesty International. We don't take government money for our research or advocacy.

These would all be constructive, welcome steps. You may not win any thanks from President Putin, but I can assure you, as a representative of the world's largest grassroots human rights organization, that your efforts can make a difference in the lives of Nadia, Masha, Sapiyat, Ghera, and countless other brave citizens of Russia who would will benefit if the U.S. Senate makes a firm commitment to advancing human rights at home and abroad.

[EDITOR'S NOTE.—The attachments to Mr. Jannuzi's prepared statement can be found in the "Additional Materials Submitted for the Record" section at the end of this hearing.]

Senator BOXER. Thank you. I thought you gave us some very good ideas.

Next, we welcome Dr. Leon Aron, of the American Enterprise Institute.

Welcome, sir.

**STATEMENT OF LEON ARON, RESIDENT SCHOLAR AND DIREC-
TOR OF RUSSIAN STUDIES, AMERICAN ENTERPRISE INSTI-
TUTE, WASHINGTON, DC**

Mr. ARON. Thank you very much, Madam Chairwoman, Ranking
Senator Johnson, Senators Paul and Murphy.

In the summer of 2011, Dan Vajdic and I were fortunate to travel
from Vladivostok to Kaliningrad across Russia to interview leaders
and activists of nongovernmental organizations and movements.
The conclusions from more than 40 hours of interviews and over
300 pages of transcripts are in this report, titled "A Quest for
Democratic Citizenship," which I ask to be entered to the record,
subject to format rules and regulations.

I recall this report because I want to put causes and faces on the
tragedy—and it is a tragedy—that is unfolding in Russia today.

These were among the finest men and women I have met anywhere. They were fearless, hardworking, smart, and absolutely
unyielding in their quest for fairness and justice. None of these
organizations and movements were political, overtly or covertly.
What united them was the moral imperative of dignity in democratic citizenship, including, first and foremost, equality before the
law and the end of effective disenfranchisement. In that, they were
not different from the civil rights movement in the United States
or the Arab Spring or the cause of the Chinese dissidents today.

All of the organizations I visited—and I keep in touch with all
of them—are now under pressure and harassment. One of them,
the Baikal Ecological Wave, which, for many years, has been trying
to save the world's largest body of freshwater from pollution, is facing the same humiliating choice as the hundreds of other nongovernmental organizations of Russia. To register as alleged foreign agents because the only support they could get is from foreign
environmental organizations will close down and abandon its cause
for good.

Looking ahead, let me mention three major implications of the
crackdown on civil society in Russia today. I will list them in the
order of growing importance, from short-term and to long-term
impacts.

First, the prospects for better United States-Russian relations
seem bleak. Any substantive reset with the United States would
contradict the regime's dominant domestic narrative of propaganda
and repression in which the United States is featured as the key
alleged threat to Russian security and domestic stability. It is possible, of course, that the regime would try and combine repression
with détente. It happened before. But, this Kremlin does not seem
to be in the mood for sophisticated bifurcation of its domestic and
foreign policies.

Second, a year into authoritarian consolidation following Vladimir Putin's reelection, what we are witnessing is a significant
change of the regime, from a relatively soft authoritarianism to a
much harder, more repressive, more malignant version. The harassment and self-exile of the leading Russian economist and establishment reformer, Professor Sergei Guriev, 2 or 3 weeks ago, was
another signal of the regime's moving in that direction.

The Kremlin's message to the establishment, liberal, pro-reform,
pro-democracy men and women in the elite seems to be something

like this, ''Stop criticizing the government or risk harassment, or even jail. If you don't like the deal, leave while the going is good. Those of you who choose to stay,'' in the words of the leading opposition blogger, Yulia Latynina, ''must, in all honesty, believe that the greatness of Russia lies in Vladimir Putin and that the source of protests against the great Putin can only be a world conspiracy and the 'fifth column' inside the government.''

Finally, I called it ''the tragedy.'' I called it a tragedy. And it is. The assault on civil society unfolding in Russia today is a tragedy for Russia, because nongovernmental organizations, grassroots organizations, are, first and foremost, a school of democracy. They teach personal responsibility, self-organization, peaceful dissent, compromise, solidarity, and respect for law. And what is left—and that is what is being destroyed—and what is left in the rubble are only stagnation, hatred, and radicalism. What is left is scorched earth, incapable of upholding democratic institutions when the regime falls, just as happened in the Soviet Union.

Thank you very much, Madam Chairman.

[The prepared statement of Mr. Aron follows:]

PREPARED STATEMENT OF LEON ARON

Thank you, Mr. Chairman. In the summer of 2011 I crossed Russia's 11 time zones, from Vladivostok to Kaliningrad, to interview about two dozen leaders and activists of six nongovernmental organizations and movements. The analytical conclusions from more than 40 hours of interviews and over 300 pages of transcripts, are in this report, titled ''The Quest for Democratic Citizenship'' which I ask to be entered in the record, subject to format rules and regulations.

But this was far more than a field study for me. These were among the finest men and women I've met anywhere. They were fearless, extremely hard working, smart and absolutely unyielding in their quest for dignity in democratic citizenship. None of the organizations and movements whose leaders and activists I interviewed was overtly political much less oppositional. Two of them were environmental; one was battling the destruction of historic buildings in St. Petersburg; one was concerned with road safety and the corruption of the traffic police; and two advocated honest elections and freedom of speech and demonstrations.

What united them all was the moral imperative of dignity in democratic citizenship, including, first and foremost, equality before the law and the end of effective disenfranchisement through restrictions on party registration and falsification of the election results. In these key regards, their core demands were no different from the civil rights movement in the United States or the demands of the Arab Spring or the cause of Chinese dissidents today.

I describe them here for you because I want to put causes and faces on the tragedy that is unfolding in Russia today. All of the organizations I visited are now under pressure and harassment. One of them, Baikal Ecological Wave which for many years has been trying to save the world's largest body of fresh water from pollution is facing the same choice as hundreds of other organizations: to register as a foreign agent, because the only support it gets is from foreign environmental organizations—or close down and abandon its cause.

Looking ahead, I see three main implications of this crackdown on civil society in Russia. Let me list them in the order of importance and from short term to longer time periods.

First, the prospects for U.S.-Russian relations seem bleak. Any substantive reset with the U.S. would contradict the regime's dominant domestic narrative of propaganda and repression, with the U.S. as the key alleged threat to Russian security and domestic stability. It is possible, of course, that the regime would try and combine repression with detente but it is unlikely: the Kremlin today seems in no mood for sophisticated bifurcation of its domestic and foreign policies. Dictated by the considerations of regime survival, the worsening of relations with the United States may be seen as a boost to the domestic legitimacy of the regime which presents itself as the defender of Russian sovereignty against the plotters from abroad, aided by paid traitors at home. Thus, expect no accommodation on Syria or Iran—or anything else that might be seen domestically as ''concession to the U.S.'' Indeed, even strategic nuclear arms reduction may fall victim to the same domestic political calculus despite the administration's concerted efforts to assuage Russia's concerns over the missile defense in Europe.

Second, what we are witnessing after a year of authoritarian consolidation, following Putin's reelection in March of last year, looks more and more like a significant change of the regime from a relatively softer authoritarianism to a much harder and malignant version. The harassment and self-exile of a leading Russian economist and establishment reformer Professor Sergei Guriev has signaled a unilateral renegotiation of the longstanding social compact with the liberal public opinion leaders. If previously proreform members of the establishment could write what they wanted and be safe from repression so long as they were not actively supporting political opposition, the Kremlin's message today is: You must stop public criticism of the government—or risk harassment and even jail. If you don't like the deal, leave while the going is still good. Those who chose to stay, in the words of a leading opposition blogger Yulia Latynina, "must in all honesty believe that the greatness of Russia in lies in Vladimir Putin," and that "the source of protests against the great Putin can only be a world conspiracy [by the West] and the 'fifth column' inside the government." [1]

Finally, and most damagingly in the long run, the assault on civil society is a tragedy for Russia because nongovernment organizations are, first and foremost, a school of democracy that teach personal responsibility, self-organization, peaceful dissent and compromise. Although on the personal level they detested the regime and never hid this attitude, the leaders and activists I interviewed were utterly pragmatic, ready to compromise and cooperate in the service of their cause. "Our attitude toward the government is that when we can cooperate with it, we do," a young woman in Vladivostok told me. "When we think that the regime's policies are wrong, we don't hesitate to say it openly."

This is what is being destroyed! Left in the ruble of civil society are only stagnation, hatred, and radicalism. Left behind is scorched earth, incapable of upholding democratic institutions, when this regime falls or implodes—just as happened after the fall of the Soviet Union.

Thank you Mr. Chairman. I ask that in addition to my study of civil society organizations, two recent articles of mine, published in the Washington Post and the Wall Street Journal, be entered into the record, subject to format rules and regulations.

End Notes

[1] Yulia Latynina, "Pikseli odnoy kartinki," gazeta.ru, May 31, 2013 and "Doktor, a otkuda u vas takie kartinki?" novyagazeta.ru, June 1, 2013.

[EDITOR'S NOTE.—The report "A Quest for Democratic Citizenship" submitted for the record was too voluminous to include in the printed hearing. It will be retained in the permanent record of the committee.

The Washington Post and Wall Street Journal articles can be found in the "Additional Material Submitted for the Record" section at the end of this hearing.]

Senator BOXER. Thank you.

And now we turn to Ambassador Sestanovich, who was the State Department's principal officer responsible for policy toward Russia, 1997 to 2001, and he is now at the Council on Foreign Relations.

STATEMENT OF HON. STEPHEN SESTANOVICH, SENIOR FELLOW FOR RUSSIAN AND EURASIAN AFFAIRS, COUNCIL ON FOREIGN RELATIONS, WASHINGTON, DC

Ambassador SESTANOVICH. Thank you very much. Senator Boxer, Senator Murphy, members of the committee, thank you for inviting me to join this timely and important discussion.

From the other witnesses on today's panel, you are receiving a full and informed picture of Russian political developments. It is a discouraging picture. But, the key question that this committee faces is, How should the United States respond? Let me suggest five things that we, and especially you, as Members of Congress, can do.

First, we need to stay out of the political struggle that is underway in Russia. Those who are trying to exercise their political rights to bring Russia into the European democratic mainstream are not asking us for direct assistance. They recognize that Putin wants to draw us into the middle of Russian politics because he thinks it will help him to stay on top. The United States should leave no confusion on this score. Russia's political course is for Russians to set. We may have our favorites, but we do not fund them. Sharpening the line between what we do and what we do not do can only help us.

Second, we should, at the same time, be emphatic that it is an international norm for nongovernmental organizations to be able to reach out to foreign donors. Doing so does not make them foreign agents. Claiming that they are is a crude attack on civil society that pits Russia against principles around which European countries have rallied since the end of the cold war. And not just European countries. Consider the recent resolution of the United Nations Human Rights Council, which declared that no state should, ''delegitimize activities in defense of human rights on account of the origins of funding thereto.'' When Putin has a majority against him at the United Nations, you know he is on shaky ground.

Third, even as we stay out of Russian politics, we should increase our support for civil society in Russia. Congress can take an important step in this direction by reviving consideration of a United States-Russia civil society fund. A year and a half ago, the Obama administration notified Congress of its intention to use some of the proceeds from the now liquidated U.S.-Russia Investment Fund to create such a fund. In light of recent developments, two adjustments of the administration's plan are called for. First, the amount should be bigger. Use all the proceeds, a full $162 million. And with no budgetary impact for the United States, let me add. And it should not be focused just on Russia. A fund to support civil society in all the countries of the former Soviet Union would advance American interests in this entire region.

Fourth, Congress should remind the administration that the Freedom Support Act is still on the books and that our national commitment to its goals is intact. For many years, the U.S. Agency for International Development oversaw most of the funding that Congress made possible in this area. But AID has ceased to operate in Russia. Congress should insist on hearing a credible plan from the administration for how the funds it has made available are to be spent effectively.

Fifth, we should remember that American strategy since the end of the cold war has reflected the unusual weakness of civil society in countries that were ruled, for decades, by Soviet-style dictatorships. Eventually, nongovernmental organizations of the kind that we take for granted in modern societies need to be self-sustaining. They need support from domestic donors. Congress should ask the administration what strategy it has for encouraging support for Russian NGOs from within Russia, itself.

For the past 2 years, Congress has wrestled with the question of how to modernize our support for human rights and democracy in Russia. The measures I have described, and others like them, would be a sign that we still have the ideas, the resources, and the commitment to advance our interests in this way.

Thank you.

[The prepared statement of Ambassador Sestanovich follows:]

PREPARED STATEMENT OF AMBASSADOR STEPHEN SESTANOVICH

Senator Boxer, Senator Murphy, members of the committee, thank you for inviting me to join this timely and important discussion. America's concern for the state of Russian democracy is sometimes portrayed as an intrusion into another country's affairs. The truth is different. Our concern reflects a strong commitment to partnership between the two countries. We have many reasons to hope for democratic consolidation in Russia, but one reason is perhaps more important than any other. Without it, Russian-American cooperation—which is very much in our national interest—will never take secure root.

From the other witnesses on today's panel, you will receive a full and informed assessment of Russian political developments. It is a discouraging picture. Over the past year and a half President Putin and his supporters have put in place a new strategy to restabilize their rule after the protest of 2011–2012. One key element of their strategy is to portray challengers to the status quo as instruments of foreign manipulation. This was Mr. Putin's first rhetorical jab at those who demonstrated against fraud in the parliamentary elections of December 2011. (It was Hillary Clinton, he claimed, who had ordered them into the streets.) The same impulse lives on in the new law requiring Russian NGOs to register as ''foreign agents'' if they receive any part of their funding from abroad.

There are some puzzling elements of Putin's strategy, but his political calculation is pretty obvious. He hopes to benefit by blurring the distinction between political movements and civil society. Many Russian NGOs do get support from abroad. Putin's political opponents do not. They do not need, do not want, and should not get foreign funds. Even so, if Putin can convince people that the two are one and the same—that the protesters are paid by foreigners to rally against him—then he has a better chance of keeping Russia's ''silent majority'' on his side. This is an obnoxious strategy, but it has clearly won some converts for him.

How should the United States respond? Let me suggest five things that we—and especially you as Members of Congress—can do.

First, we need to stay out of the political struggle that is underway in Russia. We are of course, inspired by the efforts of those who want to bring Russia into the European democratic mainstream. But they are not asking us for direct assistance. They recognize that Putin wants to draw us into the middle of Russian politics because he thinks it will help him to stay on top. The U.S. should leave no confusion on this score. Russia's political course is for Russians to set. We may have our favorites, but we don't fund them. Sharpening the line between what we do and what we won't do can only help us.

Second, we should be emphatic that it is an international norm for nongovernmental organizations to be able to reach out to foreign donors. Doing so does not make them ''foreign agents.'' Claiming that they are is a crude attack on civil society that pits Russia against principles around which European countries have rallied since the end of the cold war. And not just European countries. Consider the recent resolution of the U.N. Human Rights Council, which declared that no state should ''delegitimize activities in defense of human rights on account of the origins of funding thereto.'' When Putin has a majority against him at the U.N., you know he's on shaky ground.

Third, even as we stay out of Russian politics, we should increase our support for civil society in Russia. Congress can take an important step in this direction by reviving consideration of a U.S.-Russia Civil Society Fund. A year and a half ago the Obama administration notified Congress of its intention to use some of the proceeds from the now-liquidated U.S.-Russia Investment Fund to create such a fund. In light of recent development, two adjustments in the administration's plan are called for. The amount should be bigger (use all the proceeds—a full $162 million), and it should not be focused just on Russia. A fund to support civil society in all the countries of the former Soviet Union would advance American interests in this entire region.

Fourth, Congress should remind the administration that the Freedom Support Act is still on the books—and that our national commitment to its goals is intact. For many years, the U.S. Agency for International Development oversaw most of the spending that Congress made possible in this area. But AID has ceased to operate in Russia. Congress should insist on hearing a credible plan for how the funds it has made available are to be spent effectively.

Fifth, we should remember that American strategy since the end of the cold war has reflected the unusual weakness of civil society in countries that were ruled for decades by Soviet-style dictatorships. Eventually nongovernmental organizations of the kind that we take for granted in modern societies need to be self-sustaining. They need support from domestic donors. Congress should ask the administration what strategy it has for encouraging support for Russian NGOs from within Russia itself.

For the past 2 years, as it contemplated Russia's "graduation" from the Jackson-Vanik amendment, Congress has wrestled with the question of how to modernize our support for human rights and democracy in Russia. The measures I have described, and others like them, would be a sign that we still have the ideas, the resources, and the commitment to advance our interests in this way.

Senator BOXER. Thank you very much.

We turn to Dr. Ariel Cohen of the Heritage Foundation.

Welcome, sir.

STATEMENT OF ARIEL COHEN, SENIOR RESEARCH FELLOW FOR RUSSIAN AND EURASIAN STUDIES AND INTERNATIONAL ENERGY POLICY, HERITAGE FOUNDATION, WASHINGTON, DC

Mr. COHEN. Thank you, Madam Chairman, Senator Murphy, Senator Johnson, Senator Paul, ladies and gentlemen. My name is Ariel Cohen. I am senior research fellow at the Heritage Foundation and testify in private capacity.

Russia has missed its historic opportunity to build the modern, law-based society and democratic system of governance since the collapse of communism in 1991. This is for several reasons.

First, there was no lustration. In other words, members of the Communist Party, those who were in senior positions, and members of secret services were allowed to continue to rule the country.

Second, the corruption and the failure of the rule of law destroyed popular support of democracy.

Third, Russia had to fill the vacuum of ideology left behind by collapsed communism, and moved into the three pillars that we recognize from the czarist regime: autocracy, Christian Orthodox in Moscow patriarchate, and populism with nationalist overtones.

Why should we care? Why should America care? And why should Senate and U.S. Government do anything about it? The answer is that the more authoritarian and anti-United States Russia becomes, the more difficult it is to do business with the Kremlin, be it concerning the civil war in Syria, Iran sanctions, large-scale investment, or our support of American allies and friends in the former Soviet Union.

Today, as my colleagues mentioned, the best and the brightest of Russia are pushed into exile. Lenin, the founder of the Soviet state, first exiled the intellectuals and the philosophers by boatload and then the big terror came. Today, Sergei Guriev, the founder of the new school of economics and very much an establishment figure, was under pressure to leave his own country, the country where he advised, at the highest level, the Presidency, and was on the board of the largest Russian Bank, Sberbank. He had to stay in Paris because of the interrogations in the Mikhail Khodorkovsky third investigation. Khodorkovsky has been in jail for over 10 years now, and everybody expected him to be let go next year. However, the signs are, the Russian state is preparing the third kangaroo trial of Mikhail Khodorkovsky.

Another prominent figure is opposition leader, and the world chess champion, Garry Kasparov. Garry Kasparov announced that he is not going back to Russia, as well.

So, no, there are no philosophers' boats being shipped to the West with hundreds of Russian top talent, but people are choosing to stay abroad because of the fear. And I witnessed this fear this year, in April, when I was in Yekaterinburg, the location of the execution of the czar's family and a place where tens of thousands were killed in great terror. People came up to me and said, "We are afraid. Nothing is going to change for many, many years." This is the first time I hear such despair in Russia.

So, what can we do? Clearly, there are valid and compelling bilateral interests in Washington that we need to pursue, including our orderly withdrawal from Afghanistan, antiterrorism cooperation, the challenge of rising China, broadening business relationship, et cetera. This Senate, in passing the Jackson-Vanik amendment, created its own track record for defense of human rights in Russia. Such pillars of the Senate as "Scoop" Jackson and Daniel Patrick Moynihan were at the forefront of fighting for human rights in Russia.

Today, the Senate, the Presidency, and the U.S. Government at large needs to strike appropriate balance between pursuing American security interests and being true to our own values. So, what can we do? We can make a stronger case for civil freedoms for the Russian people through international broadcasting, which is in bad shape. It needs funding, needs serious reorganization, needs new talent and new content providers. We also need to revisit the Magnitsky List, which only has, now, 18 names on it. The Magnitsky List is the living memorial for the man who was murdered in a Russian jail, trying to be loyal to his American client.

We also have, as Americans, a wealth of experience to offer, be it in legislative policy, in health care, in developing investment and high tech. But, this will not happen if Russia is not going to be free. This is not going to happen if Russia continues to keep laws on books that call NGOs "foreign agents" if they take foreign funding. This is not going to happen if the definition of "treason" in the criminal law has been expanded to be something like what they had in Stalin's times.

Senator BOXER. I am going to ask you to wrap up now.

Mr. COHEN. So, it is true that it is up to the Russian people to make their country free, but it is up to us to give support and make our voice heard in support of freedom in Russia.

Thank you very much.

[The prepared statement of Mr. Cohen follows:]

PREPARED STATEMENT OF ARIEL COHEN

Chairman Murphy, Senator Johnson, ladies and gentlemen. My name is Ariel Cohen. I am a Senior Research Fellow, Russian and Eurasian Studies and International Energy Policy at The Heritage Foundation. First, I want to thank the subcommitee for inviting me to testify and hereby ask to enter my remarks in the record. Second, I would like to note that I testify in a private capacity and my testimony reflects my personal view only and should not be construed as views of The Heritage Foundation.

Russia has missed its historic opportunity to build a modern, law-based society and a democratic system of government since the collapse of communism in 1991. This is for several reasons. First of all, remnants of the Communist Party and the security services remained in positions of power. No lustration, or political cleansing of the old totalitarian system, was undertaken by the Russian people or their leaders, most of who belonged to the old regime.

The second reason for the reemergence of authoritarianism in Russia is the lack of rule of law as well as the rampant corruption that tainted the economic reform and the implementation of privatization during the 1990s, discrediting multiparty democracy and civil freedoms in the process. The Russian Communists as well as the nationalists exploited the situation, deliberately equating freedom and democracy with chaos and moral corruption.

Russia problems with stinted civil society and abysmal rule of law did not start with the collapse of communism. This is a known and systemic problem which has become a major roadblock on the road to the country's modernization. While czarist Russia had a rather weak and somewhat corrupt legal system, the Soviet Union used the law as an instrument of oppression, deliberately destroying even the smallest manifestation shoot of civil society. Stalin even sent speakers of Esperanto and philatelists to the GULAG camps.

The third reason for the weakness of open society in Russia is resurging nationalism, neoimperialism, and the state's alliance with the Orthodox Church, which harbors many xenophobic and anti-Western elements.

Taken together, these three elements have combined in Russia to produce what we see today: an illiberal regime which is inimical to civil society and hostile to the West both ideologically—rejecting the values of freedom and individual rights—and geopolitically. The predominant, state-supported political ideology in Russia today is close to what it was over 100 years ago: Russian Orthodoxy, autocracy, and populism with nationalist overtones.

Why should Americans care? And why should the Senate and the U.S. Government do anything about it? The answer is that the more authoritarian and anti-U.S. Russia becomes, the more difficult it is to do business with the Kremlin, be it concerning the civil war in Syria, Iran sanctions, large scale investment, or our support of American friends and allies in the former Soviet Union.

It is harder to get along with large authoritarian states that view the U.S. as an adversary, than it is with fellow democracies. However, not everyone in Russia is anti-American. Late-Soviet and post-Soviet Russian civil society has roots in the dissident movement which began under Stalin and was strongly influenced by three Nobel Prize winners—Andrey Sakharov, Alexander Solzhenitsyn, and Joseph Brodsky, who later became a U.S. poet-laureate. Some of the dissidents were pro-Western, while others, like Solzhenitsyn, were Russian nationalists and themselves deeply suspicious of the democratic West. Many of the dissidents provided piercing critiques of Stalinist totalitarianism and the late Soviet high authoritarian system. Some survivors of that early movement are still with us today, including the octogenarian Lyudmila Alexeeva, who recently testified on Capitol Hill.

Sakharov, Alexeeva, Mstislav Rostropovich, a prominent musician who later became conductor of the U.S. National Symphony, Natan Sharansky, who became Israeli Deputy Prime Minister and Interior Minister, and internationally renowned author, and many others played a key role in launching the dissident movement in the late 1960s and early 1970s.

With selfless dedication, and with the help of some international funding, including money provided by the U.S. taxpayer through USAID, the National Endowment for Democracy, the International Republican Institute, and National Democratic Institute, as well as private foundations, such as Krieble, Mott, McArthur, and Soros, Russian civil society went from taking its first baby steps to providing a wide array of services to hundreds of thousands of people. These include defending the civil rights of civilians and minorities in war zones, the fight against state corruption and graft, demanding protection against Russia's notorious police brutality and lawlessness, upholding the human rights of military recruits subject to systemic violence and abuse, promoting voters' rights, working to prevent HIV/AIDS and other diseases, advocating for the rights of the disabled, and many other activities. Recently, actions also focused on protecting those who were detained and arrested in the course of political protests after the 2011 Duma elections, which suffered from widespread voting fraud; as well as efforts to promote freedom of the media, including the Internet; secure prisoners' rights and highlight abuses in the courts; and to further environmental protection activities.

Civil society, human rights, and independent media activities, however, are dangerous pursuits in Russia. The crusading journalist, Anna Politkovskaya, was murdered in the entrance to her apartment building. Chechen human rights activist

Natalia Estemirova was gunned down. Anticorruption journalist and Novaya Gazeta editor Yurii Schchekochikhin was poisoned. Many journalists were beaten or killed; and anticorruption crusader, blogger and politician Alexei Navalny is awaiting trial on trumped up criminal charges of embezzlement.

The latest scandal at the heart of Russia's civil society involves a highly respected economist, the founder of the Russian Economic School, Sergey Guriev. He was interrogated by the country's top-flight Investigative Committee, the high profile investigations branch of the Interior Ministry (federal police) which effectively reports to the Kremlin. The authorities deliberately blurred Guriev's legal status in this case. He was reportedly suspected of taking money from jailed YUKOS oil company founder and regime opponent, Mikhail Khodorkovsky, in return for providing an expert opinion favorable to the businessman, who is now serving his second jail term. After jailing Khodorkovsky for a decade, the state alleges that he somehow initiated a review of his case by Presidential Human Rights Commission experts in order to shorten his 13 year sentence. The charges against Khodorkovsky are widely recognized as false. In Guriev's case, however, it is highly significant that he was a member of the inner sanctum of the Russian establishment, hardly a marginal figure. He undertook his activities on behalf of Khodorkovsky within the framework of the Presidential Human Rights and Civil Society Council. He was an advisor to former President Dmitry Medvedev; in close contact with leading economic ministers and pro-Kremlin businessmen; the dean of New Economic School and a star economics professor; and a member of the board of Sberbank, the largest Russian state-owned savings bank. Guriev's colleagues at the Human Rights Council included Tamara Morshchakova, the former Constitutional Court Justice; Mikhail Subbotin, an economist from the Higher School of Economics, and other prominent establishment figures.

After Guriev realized that he and his wife were being followed both in person and electronically, he fled Russia and now resides in France. In a media interview, he said that "Paris is better than Krasnokamensk" (the East Siberian town where Khodorkovsky's former labor camp is located). The charges against Guriev may have been part of an effort to launch a third Khodorkovsky trial in which, this time, the businessman would stand accused of using his funds to influence the Russian expert community in his favor. Khodorkovsky's decades-long string of prosecutions is a litmus test of Russian civic development, as he funded the liberal opposition Yabloko party, the Open Russia NGO, and other nonprofit organizations and activities, including an orphanage and an Internet training program, which connected millions of Russian schoolchildren with the outside world.

Khodorkovsky's 2003 arrest and two jail terms marked a retreat from civil liberties and a turning away from the period of relatively free political activities, and sent a resounding message to the business community to stay away not just from politics, but from civic activism. Even those who limited themselves to charities and buying Faberge eggs for the state museums are now under attack, as has been the case of Victor Vekselberg for the thankless job he did of spearheading the multibillion dollar Skolkovo high-tech park, which was supposed to recreate the Silicon Valley experience Russian style: top to bottom.

With independent TV channels coming under state control in 2000–2001, and the oligarchs Vladimir Gusinsky and the late Boris Berezovsky were pushed into exile around the same time, Russian TV channels came under state control. With democratic opposition parties effectively prevented from entering the Duma since 2004, Russian civic society and its NGOs, many of them U.S.- and Western-supported, were a breath of fresh air in the increasingly oppressive country. However, their funding within Russia was severely limited as Moscow never bothered to make the support of NGOs fully tax-exempt, and instead offered to provide government funding to friendly organizations, effectively undermining their independence.

It took almost 10 years to gradually tighten the screws—despite the Bush administration's earnest attempts to collaborate with the Kremlin over Afghanistan and Iran. Then came the much-touted "reset" policy of the Obama administration, which despite offering Russia unprecedented concessions, including a strategic nuclear weapons START treaty; freezing ballistic missile defense modernization in Europe; and a much lower profile for U.S. ties and activities in the former Soviet Union, nevertheless failed to protect Russia's civil society. Instead, the Obama administration attempted to redefine U.S. support of civil society in Russia as financing mostly nonpolitical efforts, like infant health and other health care projects. In vain.

Coming back to current developments, the Guriev affair typifies all that is wrong with the crackdown on civil society and the lack of rule of law in Russia. The authorities are generating pressure on the best and the brightest to leave. Instead of creating conditions for electoral pluralism, political party-building, the thriving nongovernmental sector, and free media, the state is doing exactly the opposite.

Some may blame it on the oil and gas windfall, as many petro-states, for example Venezuela, as well as the Middle Eastern states, are stuck between authoritarianism and populism.

The Russian leadership today rejects the freedom- and law-based Western liberal democratic model, and is increasingly pushing Russia in the direction of authoritarianism. It is no accident that some of the world's most prominent authoritarian regimes are Russia's best friends, including Cuba, Iran, Nicaragua, Syria, Venezuela, not to mention the authoritarian former Soviet republics such as Belarus and Tajikistan. Others, such as Sunni Arab monarchies, while clashing with Russia over Syria, share the regime's oil and gas revenue dependence as a distinguishing characteristic. And while former President and current Prime Minister, Dmitry Medvedev, and his advisors at least paid lip service to individual rights, professing that "Freedom is better than no freedom" and voicing tentative suggestions for political and "economic" prisoner amnesty, election of Governors and Senators in Russia's parliamentary upper house, and lowering of the minimal electoral barrier for the Duma to 5 percent, today the state's actions speak louder than any words.

While President Putin was elected last spring with a viable majority, some election fraud occurred, especially in the North Caucasus. Some Presidential candidates were not allowed to run, and those who did had no equal access to television, their funding was severely constrained, and the Central Electoral Commission chaired by Vladimir Churov, a Putin loyalist, successfully prevented a runoff. Today, the legitimacy of the current administration is questioned by many in Russia, and increasingly relies on the rural/small town, older, less educated, more nationalist and more traditional population, many of whom do not care about civil liberties and are deeply suspicious of the West.

It is against this background that we need to view the the 78-page report by Human Rights Watch (HRW), "Laws of Attrition: Crackdown on Russia's Civil Society After Putin's Return to the Presidency," which highlights some of the anti-NGO legislation and tactics that marked the return of Putin to the Presidency in May

This included the introduction of a series of law severely restricting civil society, and particularly, the activities of NGOs. It also featured the imprisonment of a number of political activists, and the characterization of the government critics as foreign-supported enemies. The HRW report analyzes these new laws, including the so-called "foreign agents" law, the treason law, and the public demonstration/assembly law, and documents how these have been used. The package of new laws and government harassment are "pushing civil society activists to the margins of the law," notes Hugh Williamson, Europe and Central Asia Director at HRW, "the government crackdown is hurting Russian society and harming Russia's international standing." [2] Many of these new measurements and activities violate Russia's international human rights commitments.

In today's Russia, draconian limits have been placed on association with foreigners and foreign funding. The term "foreign agents" deliberately hearkens back to the Stalin era, and the law requires organizations that receive foreign funding and supposedly engaged in any vaguely defined "political activities" to register as "foreign agents." Another law, adopted in December 2012, essentially bans funding from the United States for "political" activity by nongovernmental organizations, along with groups whose work is "directed against Russia's interests." Russia also shut down the activities of USAID, terminated the successful Nunn-Lugar program to dismantle weapons of mass destruction and boost nonproliferation, and caused organizations such as the International Republican Institute to relocate its staff to Lithuania.

Yet another recently passed Russian law expands the legal definition of treason in such a way that it can be used to criminalize involvement in human rights advocacy, including work for international organizations. It can also criminalize scientific and business activities involving foreigners and Russian citizens, having a chilling effect on investment and international cooperation. A recent piece of legislation effectively criminalizes unauthorized demonstrations, including their preparation, organization, and promotion, by establishing jail terms and huge fines for organizers and participants.

Since the spring of this year, the Russian authorities began a nationwide campaign of intrusive government inspections of the offices of hundreds of civil organizations. Officials from the prosecutor's office, the Justice Ministry, the tax inspectorate, and in some cases the antiextremism division of the federal police, the health inspectorate, and the fire inspectorate, have descended on the offices of election-observation NGO Golfs, Memorial, which is organizing a memorial to Stalin's victims, and even some bird sanctuaries and health advocacy organizations. The inspection campaign, which began in March 2013, was prompted by the "foreign agents" law.

Although many organizations have not received their inspection results yet, a few received citations for failing to register as "foreign agents," and others have been fined for fire safety and air quality violations and the like. According to Human Rights Watch, government inspectors examined each group's tax, financial, registration, and other documents. In several cases, they seized computers or e-mail. In one case, officials demanded that an organization prove that its staff had had been vaccinated for smallpox, and in another the officials asked for chest x-rays of staff to ensure they did not have tuberculosis. In yet another case, officials demanded copies of all speeches made at the group's recent seminars and conferences. This is clearly an unwarranted and systematic persecution of civic organizations, and particularly, of human rights organizations and activists. Such state activity goes beyond acceptable international practice and suggests that Russia, while not yet in the ranks of most oppressive human rights violators, such as Iran, North Korea, Saudi Arabia, and Cuba, is on a very worrisome trajectory.

While the Russian Government has asserted that these inspections are routine, they are clearly not. As Human Rights Watch points out, "The campaign is unprecedented in its scope and scale, and seems clearly aimed at intimidating and marginalizing civil society groups. This inspection campaign can potentially be used to force some groups to end advocacy work, or to close them down."

Currently, there are several cases of prosecution which suggest strong political motivation. These include the Guriev case discussed previously; the charges against politicians Alexei Navalny and Boris Nemtsov; and the case of the May 6 Bolotnaya Square demonstrators, with over 20 accused. Garry Kasparov, a world chess champion and one of the leaders of the Russian opposition has announced his forced emigration. He is not going back to the country, which he represented in international chess battles because he, too, like Guriev, is being called to prosecutor's office, which violates dues process and goes out of its way to destroy the peaceful opposition in Russia. Vladimir Lenin, the founder of the Soviet state, exiled philosophers and other scholars by shipload. Today, the state forces its best and brightest, like Guriev and Kasparov, to emigrate, while others, like Navalny, are threatened with jail and the GULAG camps.

There are others, such as the matter of Pussy Riot—three female punk band members who are incarcerated in labor camps for 2 years for allegedly offending the feelings of Christian Orthodox believers when their anti-Putin song was performed, admittedly in very bad taste, in Moscow's Cathedral of Christ the Savior.

Thorough investigation and research of these cases by Russian and Western experts and journalists demonstrate a lack of regular due process, biased judges and prosecutors who disregard the law, questionable and underqualified government experts, and the lack of a proper appeals process independent of the executive branch and politics. As in the Soviet past, judges bow before secret police and law enforcement and are enforcers of the political leadership's will. Most importantly, it appears that the old Soviet practice of "telephone law" is back, under which the executive authority informally and without a paper trail or track record, dictates how judges should rule in cases of particular interest.

While the Putin regime has been ratcheting up the pressure on Russian NGOs and civil activities, the Obama administration has toned down its protests against lawlessness and the crackdown on civil society in Russia. Clearly, there are valid and compelling bilateral interests that Washington and Moscow need to pursue, including an orderly withdrawal from Afghanistan; antiterrorism cooperation (the urgency for which the horrific Boston marathon bombing amply demonstrated); the search for a diplomatic settlement to the Syrian civil war; further and more effective sanctions on Iran; the challenge of rising China; and broadening business relations, especially in the energy field. Nevertheless, the U.S. should remain true to its values and protect those who seek human dignity and freedom. Speaking up for victims of oppression in the Soviet Union and Russia has a glorious history which goes back to at least the 1960s, when American Senators like "Scoop" Jackson passed the Jackson-Vanick amendment. All of us fondly remember Daniel Patrick Moynihan, a great critic of Communist excesses when he was President Ford's U.N. Ambassador and later the Senator from New York. Americans supported Andrey Sakharov, gave refuge to Alexander Solzhenitsyn, and marched in the hundreds of thousands on behalf of Soviet Jews who yearned to be free to emigrate.

Some of those who have fallen victim to the more recent crackdown are alive: Khodorkovsky, Navalny, the prisoners of the last year's Bolotnaya Square protests. Their voices need to be heard. Some are dead, like Sergey Magnitsky, Anna Politkovskaya, and Natalia Estemirova. The lives, and the reasons for their deaths, need to be remembers. Their murderers need to be apprehended and brought to justice.

Russia's civic organizations are in the process of shutting down, and one can only hope and pray that darkness won't descend. Without groups such as Golos and Memorial, without the Committee of Soldiers' Mothers, without a free media, Russia can only become more nationalist, more authoritarian, more anti-Western, and more anti-American.

The Senate, the Presidency the U.S. Government, the U.S. nonprofit sector, all need to strike a proper balance between pursuing American security, diplomatic, and business interests—and being true to our values. We need to make the support of freedom and individual rights in Russia, as well as in other places around the world where civil rights are violated or people are oppressed, a priority—as well as in this country. In our contacts with Russian officials, we need to keep bringing up the cases of those whose murderers are unsolved, or who are rotting in camps and jails. We may need to revisit the Magnitsky list, which the administration went out of its way to minimize. We need to use the power of public diplomacy, and especially international broadcasting, currently moribund for lack of new technologies and high quality content providers, to make the U.S. voice heard in Russia and other languages, from Brest to Vladivostok. America needs to make a strong case for civic freedoms to the Russian people and to the Russian leaders, and it is up to the Kremlin and to the Russian people to allow their country to move toward unencumbered political expression, a thriving civil society, and away from stagnation and authoritarianism.

America is capable of global leadership when it believes in itself and in its values. We can offer the Russian people so much—in areas they need most: to improve their uncompetitive education, abysmal health care, and chilling investment climate. We can expand space cooperation, energy exploration, and work together on much-needed infrastructure development in that vast country that covers nine time zones.

Most importantly, U.S. have a wealth of experience to offer in legislative policy, court administration and—despite the recent scandals—the rule of law. The good will is there, but Russia would need an unencumbered nonprofit sector and the rule of law to benefit from it.

It is up to the Russian leadership to rise to the challenge, to allow the nonprofit sector to thrive, and to restore cooperation with the U.S. The ball is in Moscow's court.

End Notes

[1] "Laws of Attrition: Crackdown on Russia's Civil Society after Putin's Return to the Presidency," Human Rights Watch, April 24, 2013, http://www.hrw.org/reports/2013/04/24/laws-attrition.
[2] Ibid.

Senator BOXER. Thank you so much.

And finally, we hear from Boris Nemtsov. In addition to being a former Deputy Prime Minister of Russia, he is cochairman of what I believe is the opposition party, the Republican Party of Russia–People's Freedom Party, and, in January 2011, he was sentenced to 15 days in jail after taking part in an opposition rally.

We are very happy to have you here, sir. Please go ahead.

STATEMENT OF HON. BORIS NEMTSOV, COCHAIRMAN OF REPUBLICAN PARTY OF RUSSIA–PEOPLE'S FREEDOM PARTY, MOSCOW, RUSSIA

Mr. NEMTSOV. Well, thank you very much for opportunity to be with you today.

I want to thank you for holding this timely and topical hearing and for giving me the opportunity to share my views on the situation in Russia.

I want to tell you that I have a ticket to Moscow today, and—100 percent, I will be back, and—but, I think that opposition leaders must fight inside the country, not outside.

With Vladimir Putin's return to the Presidency in May 2012, Russia's authoritarian regime has transitioned to a new stage of development, from so-called "sovereign democracy," characterized by election fraud, media censorship, and the harassment of the opposition, to open political repression. Critics of Mr. Putin's government, from opposition leaders to rank-and-file activists, are being put up for political show trials.

The case of the participants of the May 2012 anti-Putin rally, the so-called "Bolotnaya case," the case of anticorruption campaigner Alexei Navalny, and the possible third criminal case, which Ariel mentioned, against Mikhail Khodorkovsky, Russia's most prominent political prisoner, are only some of the examples of a rapidly worsening situation.

Meanwhile, new laws targeting the freedom of assembly, expanding the definition of "treason," and labeling NGOs that receive funding from abroad as "foreign agent," which, in Russian language, is synonymous with "foreign spies," show that the regime is no longer satisfied with mere political control and seeks to subject society to fear and submission.

In this context, attempts by some in the West, including in the United States, to adopt a realpolitick approach and to conduct business as usual with the Putin regime, contradict the most basic values of democracy, human rights, and the rule of law. Such policy is also counterproductive, since the Kremlin considers it as a sign of weakness and, therefore, as an invitation to behave even more aggressively, both at home and abroad.

This coming Monday, G8 leaders, including Barack Obama and Vladimir Putin, will gather for a summit in Northern Ireland. The agenda does not even include any mention of human rights abuses in Russia. The G8 is still known as the group of leading industrial democracies, which sounds incredibly grotesque, given the situation in Russia. It would be more appropriate, and more honest, to refer to the group as "G7 plus Putin."

Last year, the U.S. Congress adopted the most pro-Russian law in the history of any foreign Parliament, including the U.S. Congress. The Magnitsky Act, directed against crooks and abusers, finally ends the impunity for those who violate the rights and steal the money of Russian citizens. According to a recent poll—Russian recent poll—by the Levada Center, 44 percent of Russian people support the Magnitsky Act, with just 21 percent against and 35 percent holding no opinion. And this, despite the massive Kremlin propaganda against this law.

Unfortunately, the initial public list of violators that was published by the U.S. administration in April includes only 18 names, none of them high-ranking. Too many of those responsible for repression and human rights abuses have been let off the hook. This is a great strategic error. I hope that it will be corrected in the near future.

It is our task, the task of Russian citizens, to bring about democratic changes in our country. This cannot be done from outside. But, if the United States wants to show support for the Russian people, the best way to do it is also to implement the Magnitsky Act, in full accordance with the original intent.

Thank you very much.

[The prepared statement of Mr. Nemtsov follows:]

PREPARED STATEMENT OF HON. BORIS NEMTSOV

Chairwoman Boxer, Chairman Murphy, Ranking Member Paul, Ranking Member Johnson, esteemed members of the committee, I want to thank you for holding this timely and topical hearing and for giving me the opportunity to share my views on the situation in Russia.

With Vladimir Putin's return to the Presidency in May 2012, Russia's authoritarian regime has transitioned to a new stage of development—from the "sovereign democracy" characterized by election fraud, media censorship, and the harassment of the opposition, to overt political repression. Critics of Mr. Putin's government—from opposition leaders to rank-and-file activists—are being put up for political show trials. The case of the participants of the May 2012 anti-Putin rally (the so-called "Bolotnaya case"); the case of anticorruption campaigner Alexei Navalny, and the possible third criminal case against Mikhail Khodorkovsky, Russia's most prominent political prisoner, are only some of the examples of a rapidly worsening situation. Meanwhile, new laws targeting the freedom of assembly, expanding the definition of "treason," and labeling NGOs that receive funding from abroad as "foreign agents," (which in Russian is synonymous with "foreign spies") show that the regime is no longer satisfied with mere political control and seeks to subject society to fear and submission.

In this context, attempts by some in the West, including in the United States, to adopt a realpolitik approach and to conduct "business as usual" with the Putin regime contradict the most basic values of democracy, human rights and the rule of law. Such policy is also counterproductive, since the Kremlin considers it as a sign of weakness—and, therefore, as an invitation to behave even more aggressively, both at home and abroad.

This coming Monday, G8 leaders—including Barack Obama and Vladimir Putin—will gather for a summit in Northern Ireland. The agenda does not include any mention of human rights abuses in Russia. The G8 is still known as the group of leading industrialized democracies, which sounds increasingly grotesque given the situation in Russia. It would be more appropriate to refer to the group as "G7 plus Putin."

Last year, the U.S. Congress adopted the most pro-Russian law in the history of any foreign Parliament. The Magnitsky Act, directed against crooks and abusers, finally ends the impunity for those who violate the rights and steal the money of Russian citizens. According to a recent poll by the Levada Center, 44 percent of Russians support the Magnitsky Act (with just 21 percent against, and 35 percent holding no firm opinion)—and this despite the massive Kremlin propaganda.

Unfortunately, the initial public list of violators that was published by the U.S. administration in April includes only 18 names—none of them high-ranking. Too many of those responsible for repression and human rights abuses have been let off the hook. This is a grave strategic error. I hope that it will be corrected in the nearest future.

It is our task—the task of Russian citizens—to bring about democratic changes in our country. This cannot be done from outside. But if the U.S. wants to show solidarity with the Russian people, the best way to do it is to implement the Magnitsky Act in full accordance with its original intent.

Senator BOXER. And thank you for your courage. And I would just say, you know, on behalf of all of us, your being here helps shine the light on what is happening, and I hope that—because we now know you and we now know what you face, that, when you get back there, you will have respect and not be mistreated. And we certainly will follow that very closely.

I want to start the questions with Mr. Jannuzi. I thought you gave us two really important ideas. One is to keep shining the light on these abuses, which is always very effective, I think. And, second, you said, before the President goes to his summit meeting—is it called a summit?—in September——

Mr. JANNUZI. In September, there will be a summit meeting in Moscow.

Senator BOXER [continuing]. A summit meeting that we need to, if we can, put human rights on the agenda, which we have learned is not on the agenda. So, what I am going to work with, with Senator Johnson, Senator Murphy, Senator Paul, is a bipartisan letter that we can send to the administration, saying that we are very concerned, and perhaps sending them a summary of this hearing, so they can—and we will send that to John Kerry, as well. And I think that would be a good way to show bipartisan support for putting this on the agenda and not letting it be swept under the rug. Do you think that would make some sense?

Mr. JANNUZI. I do, Senator. I've always felt that human rights should not be an afterthought in summitry, that human rights issues are really integral to everything else the United States is trying to accomplish, whether it is with Russia or with China or other great powers. And, by signaling that intention, I think we put the Russians on notice that we care.

Senator BOXER. And perhaps it is up to the—I think we will talk about it—maybe we will want to see Secretary of State Kerry, or at least do a conference call with him, where we can underscore this, because one of the things I was struck by, both by comments up here and out there, is, you know, we really do not know exactly where this is all leading. And it could be leading to a horrible place—it is already in a very bad place—and may not be. But, it is one of those moments when, if there is any thought process going on over there, that they need to understand that people are watching.

Ambassador, I wanted to ask you to expand on your suggestions to us. You said, ''Congress should remind the administration that the Freedom Support Act is still on the books, our national commitment to its goals is intact, and, for many years, AID oversaw most of the spending that Congress made in this area, but AID has ceased to operate in Russia. Congress should insist on hearing a credible plan for how the funds it has made available are to be spent effectively.''

Can you give us a sense of—you know, you are saying Congress should insist on hearing a credible plan. What would a credible plan be, to you, if you had the opportunity to give input into that?

Ambassador SESTANOVICH. Well, thank you for the opportunity to elaborate that point, Senator, because I think resources are just as important as letters, and create facts on the ground and capabilities in Russian civil society that may not otherwise exist.

AID has had the lead in spending money through a variety of organizations that it has supported over the years. I think it probably may be in the ballpark, this year, of $40–$50 million in democracy-in-governance support. But, that is now an empty vessel. AID is closing up shop. And the question is, What will happen to that amount of money? where will it go? who will have control over it in the U.S. Government? Or are we just going to take the fact that AID has been closed down by the Russian Government as a reason that the United States Government cannot do anything in this area?

There is a debate going on, in the administration, about how to dispose of those funds and who should have control over them. And I cannot settle the question for you here, but I think the crucial question is whether the United States stays interested in this issue and puts resources behind its interest.

There are some people who are saying, really we cannot do anything in this area, so we should shift to other activities. I think that would be a mistake, for all the reasons——

Senator BOXER. Well, give me an example. If you were sitting in the room, and had—just give us one example. You say we should insist on a credible plan. So, I am asking you, Assuming we could find someone to execute the plan, what would be some of the top ideas you would have?

Ambassador SESTANOVICH. Well, as I say, it always matters who is able to dispose of the money and what kinds of groups can be——

Senator BOXER. But, I am asking you.

Ambassador SESTANOVICH [continuing]. Supported. Yes.

Senator BOXER. You are an expert. What are your ideas?

Ambassador SESTANOVICH. I think there are many different organizations in Russia that are worthy of support. My copanelists have mentioned environmental groups, have mentioned groups interested in public health. But, I would focus on a couple that I think are particularly at the interface between civil society and politics. And I will give you two. Two kinds of activities. I am not going to give you specific donors.

Senator BOXER. That is fine.

Ambassador SESTANOVICH. One involves polling and public opinion, the other involves election monitoring.

The Russian Government has tried to create the idea that these are political activities, and that any groups involved in these activities are political actors, as though people who count the ballots in an election are engaged in political activity instead of creating a fair playing field. So, polling groups and election monitors have come under particular pressure. These are critical functions. And whatever the mechanism that we pursue for supporting activities of that kind, we should——

Senator BOXER. Well, that is very——

Ambassador SESTANOVICH [continuing]. Definitely take——

Senator BOXER [continuing]. That is very helpful. And I saw Mr. Jannuzi shaking his head yes, and I saw Mr. Cohen——

Mr. JANNUZI. Just strong affirmation.

Senator BOXER. So, that would be the strong affirmation.

And, Mr. Cohen, do you agree with that idea, about polling and that—but, you shook your head when he said ''environmental groups.'' I saw that.

Mr. JANNUZI. Yes.

Senator BOXER. Mr. Cohen.

Mr. COHEN. Yes. I think the battlefield today is not in health care. I witnessed, during the Obama administration—Secretary Clinton came and opened civil society, Congress here, and it was inundated with health care and other noncontroversial——

Senator BOXER. Yes.

Mr. COHEN [continuing]. U.S.-supported, taxpayer-supported activities. It did not work. The crackdown on American civil society activities came after that, not before that.

So, this—I do not want to use a word like ''appeasement,'' but it did not work, and the battlefield is in what my colleague Steve Sestanovich said: transparency. Clear—clean elections——

Senator BOXER. Good.

Mr. COHEN [continuing]. Clean politics, whistleblowing. Alexei Navalny is facing five criminal cases. Alexei Navalny is the leading whistleblower in Russia. So, yes, we should support, we should focus, but, no, we should not shy from the battle.

Thank you.

Senator BOXER. Thank you.

My time is up, so I am going to turn to Senator Johnson.

Senator JOHNSON. Thank you, Madam Chair.

And, by the way, I would fully support an effort to, you know, put a letter together prior to the summit. And from my standpoint, I would personally call on members of this distinguished panel to provide me the input, provide this panel the input, this committee the input, on what the prioritized listing of issues we should put in the letter, as well as the individuals that we should call out, the people of courage, like Mr. Nemtsov, you know, to make sure that the Russians know that we are watching and, you know, we want to make sure that these people are treated with human dignity and respect.

Two people mentioned the Magnitsky List, that we only have 18 individuals listed on that. Without naming the people, I would like to know who—you know, I would also like to know your version of who should be on the list, but can you tell us how many people should be on that list? Should it be thousands, should it be hundreds? I mean, what—to have main effect.

Mr. Cohen, you mentioned it.

Mr. COHEN. Thank you, Senator.

On a case-by-case basis, and with examination of proper evidence, I would say there should be a process that selects these individuals. I will not venture a number right now. I think you have to look at who was involved in what kind of activities. And the language of the law does not limit it to the case of the late Sergei Magnitsky. The language of the law expands the scope of the law to address systematic, gross violations of human rights and economic activities that stem from those abuses. And with this criteria, these individuals should be evaluated and then entered into the list.

Senator JOHNSON. Well, obviously, this administration did not follow criteria to add enough people, according to you folks, or at least a couple of you, in terms of people on that list. So, what should be the process? I mean, is that something you could also feed into this committee, in terms of who should be on that list?

Mr. Aron, would you like to——

Mr. ARON. Well, I actually defer to Boris Nemtsov.

Senator JOHNSON. Okay.

Mr. ARON. I think he is the best expert on this.

Senator JOHNSON. Mr. Nemtsov.

Mr. NEMTSOV. Well, first of all, I want to tell that the administration has already got a lot of names, which was prepared by a human rights organization from Russia and from the United States. My understanding is that they do not want to be serious, as far as this list is concerned. They want to be very cautious, because they are afraid of Putin disappointment and his aggression, et cetera, et cetera. I think that this is great mistake——

Senator JOHNSON. So, how many people are on that list?

Mr. NEMTSOV. Well, I want to tell you that there are several lists which were prepared by NGO. One is very short, about 13 names; another looks bigger, about 200 names. I do not think that you must think about an amount of names; I think that most important thing, like Ariel said, and that is that people who are responsible for violation of law, people who are responsible for political repression in Russia, must be included, nevertheless what there is a relationship between these guys and Putin.

Senator JOHNSON. Okay. So, you want the right names on the list, as do I, so I would like to work with you, in terms of getting those people on that list.

Let me talk a little bit about—or, I would like to get your input on the effect of the reset, or, even more so, the effect on U.S. policy, or lack of policy, in terms of emboldening Putin. I am exactly sure who I should ask that question to, so whoever—it looks like—you know, whoever wants to answer that. What is that effect, in terms of, really, the deteriorating civil society in Russia? America's lack of leadership.

Mr. Aron.

Mr. ARON. Well, I think—you know, depending on who you speak to, the reset had either very specific goals or very broad goals. I think it was oversold as a kind of, you know, broader coincidence of values in some areas. Others were more realistic about it and felt that this is just about arms control.

Now, this administration continues to pursue another arms control—or, I should say, arms reduction agreement with Russia. It pursues it, I think, with a great deal of zeal, thus giving, I think, the Kremlin what they at least interpret as the ability to manipulate the relationship because the administration wants an arms control deal. This is something to watch for. This is not the cold war, this is not the Soviet Union. The pursuit of arms control cannot be a be-all and an excuse-all kind of policy. And I think this is where, not just a reset, but the broader structure of our relationship needs to be somewhat corrected.

Senator JOHNSON. Mr. Sestanovich.

Ambassador SESTANOVICH. Senator, I think there are pluses and minuses to their reset record. And one could go through, issue by issue, and evaluate them. But, if the question is, ''Did something in the reset trigger Putin's repression?'' I would give you a different answer. I would say the calculation that Putin made was based primarily on the appearance, unexpected for him, of an amazing degree of popular opposition and the readiness of people in Moscow and other cities across Russia to go into the streets and demonstrate against electoral fraud, against him. That challenge is one that I think he would have responded to, in the way that he has, no matter what kind of Russian-American relationship you created.

Senator JOHNSON. Okay.

Ambassador SESTANOVICH. Because his instincts are what they are.

Senator JOHNSON. Thank you.

Ambassador SESTANOVICH. He is——

Senator JOHNSON. I am running out of time, and I want to get to one conflict that I heard.

Mr. Sestanovich, you said we need to stay out of Russia. Mr. Jannuzi, you said we need to shine the spotlight. Are those mutually exclusively? Or—you know, I just kind of wanted to get that—I think spotlight's good, but in what——

Mr. JANNUZI. Senator, I think I can square that circle.

The strongest proponents of human rights—basic rights, civil rights—in the world do not live along the banks of the Potomac, they live along the banks of the Volga, the Amur, and other rivers, you know, in Russia. And by shining a spotlight on their efforts, by supporting, both rhetorically and, as Ambassador Sestanovich has said, to the extent we are able, through training initiatives and civil society promotion, activities, supporting their efforts, we are not intruding into the decisionmaking of the Russian people; we are helping them have the tools they need to make those decisions for themselves in a more democratic, open, and transparent way. And so, I believe that we can do both.

Senator JOHNSON. Mr. Cohen, you raised your hand, there.

Mr. COHEN. We, at the Heritage Foundation, documented the failure of the reset policy. I can point out one success, and that is cooperation on the United States transportation network into Afghanistan, and now out of Afghanistan. Other than that: Syria, missile defense; Iran, terrorism. It did not work. In case of anti-terrorism cooperation, it did not work well enough. To wit, Boston.

I think that the issues at hand—civil society, human rights—should remain on the table. It is our national security interest—it was so since Jimmy Carter, since Ronald Reagan—that Russia will move into the direction of freedom, civil society, and cooperation. The more Russia goes there, the better it is for the Russian people. They are talking about lack of sustainability of the current economic model that is based on oil and gas. Well, you develop your non-natural resources economy by having a freer society, by having your elites staying in Russia, living in Russia, working in Russia, and creating wealth there and not in New York, although I am not against the fact that they are contributing to the welfare and prosperity of this great country.

Thank you.

Senator JOHNSON. Thank you, Mr. Cohen.

I guess I will turn it over to the new chair.

Senator MURPHY. Thank you, Senator Johnson.

I wanted to further explore the comment that Ambassador Sestanovich raised, which is that Putin's turn toward repression comes from a fear of a changing level of opposition from the Russian people. And I guess I will start with Mr. Nemtsov with this question. I would love your thoughts, and then others, as to the status of popular opinion in Russia today with respect to this level of oppression. We saw a high level of organized unrests in 2011, in 2012. We have not seen as much organized protest and unrest this year as we have in previous years. And I guess the simple question, to start with you, Mr. Nemtsov, and then others want to chime in, is, Is this because the tactics have succeeded and there is a similar amount of opposition to Putin today than there has been in the past, and people just feel like they cannot express that? Or is there less interest than we might otherwise think amongst the Russian people in this new series of oppressive and repressive tactics?

Mr. NEMTSOV. Well, first of all, Putin lost, after the election—after the election of 2012—he lost more than 10 percent. Secondly, in authoritarian country, public opinion is very strange thing, because public opinion formed by TV, mainly, in Russia—more than 65 percent of Russians get information from TV, not from Internet. And TV is under 100 percent of Putin control. That is why, for example, Russian people do not like America—not because they think that this is devil empire, but because Putin TV show that this is our enemy. That is it. That is why this is manipulation, this is not public opinion, in democratic understanding point of view.

Well, people are tired of him. People know that he is a leader of corruption team. People know that he is very rich. Very rich, not because of his incomes, but because of corruption scheme, et cetera, et cetera. People know that there is new oligarchy team around him, including KGB guys, et cetera. That is why I think that his popularity is going down and down.

As far as protest is concerned, your second question, I am one of the organizer of rally and demonstrations from 2011. What the main problem. Yes, it was, yesterday, a good demonstration, with more than 20,000 of people on the streets, which is good, with this main slogan, ''Freedom for political prisoners and for free Russia and for democratic Russia,'' which is great, but people want to get results immediately. They believe that if we came to the street with 100,000 of people, Putin will disappear in 1 second. This is Russian tradition: to get result immediately. You know, if you—if you explain, them, ''Guys, this guy control 600 billion U.S. dollars in reserves,'' he is one of the richest men in the world, and he is very much afraid to be in jail, and he is ready to use every opportunity to keep his power, and I do not think that one peaceful rally is enough—it is very unpopular idea, but this is realistic.

That is why we must continue, I am 100 percent sure, because peaceful protest is an only way for Russia. Russia has terrible history of bloody revolutions, with terrible results. That is why our absolutely clear choice is to continue, but peaceful protest.

Senator MURPHY. Let me just see if there are any other quick thoughts on the status of public opinion.

Mr. JANNUZI. Senator, we do not have good polling data, but we know that, since Putin was inaugurated last year, more than 5,100 people have been arrested. This is having a chilling effect on their willingness to come out in the streets. And the fact that there were 10- to 15- or 20,000 people in the streets of Moscow yesterday, the day after the Duma had passed new restrictive laws, suggests that there is a significant amount of unrest and unhappiness. More information on this is available at our infographic at AmnestyUSA.org. And we do not see a diminution in the willingness of the Russian people to step up and criticize their government. But, the size of the protests is being reduced, out of fear.

Senator MURPHY. All right.

Mr. Cohen.

Mr. COHEN. From my sense—I am a lapsed lawyer, and one of the few things that I am dragging from my legal past is engagement in writing about the Russian Constitution. I spoke in Russia,

in Yekaterinburg, about that. And what Russian Constitution provides—I think, mistakenly—is that the Presidency is above the
three branches of government. Well, ladies and gentlemen, I am
sorry to say, the Presidency in Russia, de facto, is the executive
branch and is very politicized. The Russian Constitution says that
the President of Russia is a guarantor of the constitution. Since
2011, Mr. Putin is no longer guarantor of the constitution. Maybe
even from before that. Mr. Putin is a part of a political struggle in
Russia. He is a political actor. And he, as such, today, unfortunately for him, lost control of the Russian elites. Today, in every
poll that you see of people who are under 45, urban, and educated,
Mr. Putin's party, United Russia, is not getting the majority. And
his popularity is not growing. It used to be very high. It used to
be in the 75-percent range. Not among the elites anymore.

So, what is he doing? He is doing what any politician is doing:
disregarding the Russian Constitution and being the guarantor and
above the branches—the three branches of government, because,
between us, this is basically, a description of a czar. He is shifting
his political base to less educated, more urban and small town, and
older. And that is part of the explanation for the crackdown, for
this policy that is pulling Russia back into the past, into this populism and disregard to the rule of law.

Senator MURPHY. I will save my second few questions for the second round. Maybe we will go back to Senator Johnson now, and
then, now that Senator McCain has joined, we will give him a
chance to take a breath and ask questions after Senator Johnson.

Senator JOHNSON. Thank you, Mr. Chairman.

I just want to follow up, really, on the flow of information into
Russia. Mr. Nemtsov, you talked about 60 or 65 percent of the
information Russians get is from Russian TV, and yet we have a
fair amount of real information coming in there, to the extent
where you have got the elite that are against Putin. Where are
they getting it from? How free is the Internet? You know, how restricted is it?

Mr. NEMTSOV. Well, Internet is relatively free. Comparing, first
of all, with China or Belarus or Iran and some other countries, it
looks free, except maybe the most powerful Web sites, like
Yandex—this is Russian Google—like Mail.ru, like some others.
But, we have an opportunity to use Twitter, Facebook, to use
LiveJournal, some other Web sites.

But, I want to tell you that Internet is not targeting information
resource, because you can get, in Internet, all of the information,
from freshest, you know, to pornographia. You can get everything
you want. If you look at TV—why TV is so influential and why this
is so powerful—because this is absolutely targeting resource,
"Putin is good. McCain is disaster." That is it. [Laughter.]

Senator JOHNSON. No offense, Senator. [Laughter.]

Mr. NEMTSOV. Well, it is very clear message——

Senator JOHNSON. Welcome to the hearing.

Mr. NEMTSOV. Yes. [Laughter.]

Mr. NEMTSOV. Very clear message. But very targeted, right?
Every day, from the morning to the dark, "I am a hero, I am a
patriot, America is our main enemy, while our Russian opposition,
all of them, are American spies," including me, of course, while—

that is it. And every day. If you look at Internet, you get different information, free.

Senator JOHNSON. So, we certainly do understand the power of mainstream media, here. But, what is—what is the power—I will ask somebody else on the panel—What is the power of the alternate information? As well as—I also want to tack on this question, too, is—What is the prospect of relatively free and fair elections? I mean, how unfair are they? How easy is it for Putin to steal those, time and time again?

Mr. NEMTSOV. Let me—well——

Senator JOHNSON. Okay.

Mr. NEMTSOV. I know an answer. We do not have elections. We have special operation, always.

One example. Election—mayor election in Moscow City, the biggest city in Russia, the most opposition city, and the most well-educated city, with concentration of money, with a budget like in New York City. Well, they decided to organize these elections, just few days ago, with Putin, because of summer vacations and because of great pressure to Alexei Navalny, who is one of the candidate—he wants to take part—and because they are very afraid of Mikhail Prokhorov, Russian billionaire who wanted to take part. But, they—specially for Prokhorov, they adopted a law that all of the money and the assets must be in the country, even if you are just candidate. To Prokhorov, it means that Brooklyn Mets basketball team must be in Moscow in one week——

Senator JOHNSON. Right.

Mr. NEMTSOV [continuing]. Because he is an owner of this basketball——

Senator JOHNSON. So, you are really describing——

Mr. NEMTSOV. That is why—you know, they—they separate everybody. This——

Senator JOHNSON. Right.

Mr. NEMTSOV. Do you think that this is elections? And, as far as Navalny is concerned, you know, he face five criminal cases against him.

Senator JOHNSON. So, they are certainly not fair elections, but, again, when he gets right down to balloting, if there was more free flow of information, if they—if they were not able to rig, you know, the timing of them so there is absolutely no chance for the opposition to be known and to get traction within the public, is there a prospect for the actual election to be—represent what people are actually voting, or is it—they are always stolen?

Mr. Cohen.

Mr. COHEN. It is a matter of demographics. The demographics of, I would say, 45 or 50, and up, which is still a big demographic, get their information from TV. TV channels are controlled by the state, one way or another. But, I would like to focus your attention on what we are doing or not doing—rather, not doing—with American international broadcasting.

International broadcasting helped us to win the cold war. I am proud to be part of the Radio Liberty research that was a part of that. Today, we are not doing that anymore. We are not doing that vis-a-vis Russia, we are doing—barely doing it vis-a-vis Iran, we do not have successful and widely popular media in the Arab world.

And I am just not a specialist in China, so I—it is hard for me to compare.

We are in a different media world, we are in a different media environment, but I do not see the same fervor, the same impact, the same technology, and the same content that we managed, together with Russian emigres, together with prominent Russian intellectuals at the time, to generate. And I do believe that it was American public broadcasting that helped us to bring communism down, and that there is no reason why we cannot promote the cause of freedom today in the Muslim world and in nonfree societies.

Senator JOHNSON. Mr. Jannuzi.

Mr. JANNUZI. Senator, as important as information is—and I agree, very much, that access to accurate information is essential for an informed electorate—the problem in Russia has more to do with the ability to speak truth to power once you know that truth. It is about freedom of speech, freedom of assembly, freedom of association. So, information, great, I am all for it. But, what we really need is to be focusing on the defenders of the civic space in Russia.

Senator JOHNSON. Right. But, again, you do not have the civil rights, so is it possible to broadcast that through the Internet, through things like Radio Free Europe, I mean, those types of levers that we used to, you know, wield far better, here in the United States, than what we are apparently doing today?

Mr. JANNUZI. I think the passion and the activism is in Russia now. We do not need to ignite it through broadcasting. We need to stand with those who are attempting to wield their power.

Women like Sapiyat Magomedova, she is a human rights defender in Dagestan. She goes after police who use violence against those who they are supposed to be protecting. But, she, herself, as a human rights defender and lawyer, is now coming under death threats and scrutiny from the authorities.

Senator JOHNSON. So, we should put her in our letter.

Mr. JANNUZI. We should put her in our letter, and we will help you do that, Senator.

Senator JOHNSON. Okay.

Ambassador SESTANOVICH. Okay. Can I add one thing that—to follow up on what Frank has said? There is no doubt that the impact of the new legislation about foreign funding is having an impact on civil society groups. They are finding it harder to operate. Their budgets are under pressure. And the question for them is going to be how much foreign donors are actually pulling back from supporting them, which is why I suggested that Congress should take a look at reviving the United States-Russia civil society fund, from a year and a half ago, that the administration proposed. We have not yet seen the real contraction of activities by NGOs in Russia. But, that is coming, because they are under a lot of pressure, and they are finding it difficult to keep the resources.

So far, nobody has been convicted under this law, but that may come, too.

Senator JOHNSON. The threat is there.

Okay, I just want to say thank you all. This has been, I think, enormously helpful, certainly to me. I could sit here and ask questions for hours, and maybe we should be convening that type of panel.

But, thank you, Mr. Chairman.

Senator MURPHY. Thank you.

Senator McCain.

Senator McCAIN. Well, thank you, Mr. Chairman. I share your comment, there, that these are five of the most respected people I know, in America, that have spent, literally, their careers, four of them, in behalf of human rights. And Mr. Nemtsov has obviously been on the front line in his efforts to bring democracy back to Russia.

I would like to ask the panel about the Magnitsky Act. I would like to know its effect in Russia, whether it has been implemented in the manner which we had hoped it would be, as far as the number of people who would have been affected by it. And, third of all, do you believe that we should make the Magnitsky Act a global act from—there's many—you know, we went through a debate, when we passed this, to whether it should be global or just Russia-specific.

So, Mr. Jannuzi, maybe I could begin with you, and we will go down the line.

Mr. JANNUZI. Senator, I am hamstrung by the fact that the Amnesty International organization, because of a skepticism of the use of sanctions, took no position on the Magnitsky Act, but we strongly believe that, if you are going to have it, you ought to use it wisely. And that means that you need to be looking at the list—not only should it be accurate, but it should be calibrated to your political objectives. That list could be populated with hundreds of names, if you wanted to, based on the criteria of the law. I do not think anyone has that intention.

But, if your goal is to send that message to the decisionmakers in Russia about our commitment to human rights and our hope that they will embrace those rights, as well, then you need to calibrate the list politically. It is a political decision, how many names and which names you put on there.

Senator McCAIN. And its effect in Russia?

Mr. JANNUZI. It has pissed off President Putin greatly. [Laughter.]

We got his attention. Once you have his attention, there has to be engagement if there is going to be progress. That is why we are calling for President Obama to put human rights prominently on the agenda of his summit meeting with President Putin in September. He should raise human rights, both privately and publicly, at other opportunities, including a 1-hour meet-and-greet that he has with President Putin in Iceland. If he raises these issues consistently at a time when we have their attention, he is more likely to get a good listening.

Senator McCAIN. Mr. Aron.

Mr. ARON. Yes. Senator, I think sometimes we have to look, not just at the nitty-gritty of stuff, but at symbols. We now know, from the memoirs of the prisoners of conscience in the Soviet Union, including Anatoly, now Nathan, Shcharansky, about the enormous effect of the "Evil Empire" speech by Ronald Reagan, of the "Bring down that wall, Mr. President—Mr. General Secretary."

The effects may not be immediate, but, I think, apart from the punishment of what is known in Russia's crooks and swindlers, and the repression, I think the enormous impact of the Magnitsky Act is precisely in showing the solidarity with that quest for democratic citizenship, of which I spoke before.

I think the effect is on the urban, younger generation, whom, by the way, Putin lost, I mean, by every public-opinion poll—the future of Russia is not with his constituency. And therefore, you know, this has been a fairly gloomy session, but, short term, things are very bleak. I think—even in the medium term—I think we ought to be hopeful.

But, this expression of solidarity is extremely important, and I think the—again, apart from the specific names on that list, I would—any continuation—any continuation of attention to the Magnitsky Act and the Magnitsky process, I hope—I think is going to be, long term and even medium term, of enormous symbolic importance for those who strive for democracy and human rights in Russia.

Senator MCCAIN. Do you share Mr. Jannuzi's view of Mr. Putin's reaction? [Laughter.]

Mr. ARON. I think all kinds of acts were involved, yes. Not just the one that he mentioned.

Ambassador SESTANOVICH. Senator, I think the effect of the Magnitsky bill has been primarily symbolic. Symbolism is good. It symbolizes American commitment and interest in the rule of law in Russia. But, beyond the symbolism, I think the effect, for many members of the Russian elite, has been relief. That is, they are coming to understand that the reach of this act is relatively limited.

Senator MCCAIN. Only because of its interpretation.

Ambassador SESTANOVICH. Well, not exclusively because of its interpretation. The law says that the people on the list are those who are guilty of gross violations of human rights, and it gives two examples: killing and torture. So, that is going to limit the reach of the act.

I think you need—whatever—however you apply the Magnitsky Act, you need other elements of a modern policy to demonstrate American commitment to human rights and to put resources behind it.

So, symbolism, by itself, is good. It is not the only element of American strategy.

Senator MCCAIN. But, a step in the right direction.

Mr. Cohen.

Mr. COHEN. Senator, I think that the Magnitsky Act was used and abused by the Russian leadership, up to and including punishing orphans that were supposed to be adopted by American families, who would give them, not only warm homes, but medical care that they desperately needed. One of these orphans already died, according to the Russian media. So, the punishment of the orphans, the punishment of civil society, the slew of legislation, the crackdown, this was the message to us that we created, supposedly, more damage by promulgating the Magnitsky Act than what happened.

I do believe that we need to revisit the act. We need to see who falls into the scope of the act, and possibly expand it. This is not my decision; this is above my pay grade. This is your decision, Senators.

Senator MCCAIN. But, we value your advice.

Mr. COHEN. And I will be happy to provide the advice, of course, as will my colleagues. However, you asked a trillion-ruble question, Senator, Should it be expanded? And I would say, "Yes," with caution, because we have our foreign policy priorities that influence these kind of decisions. And I think, if you look at the Reagan era, how Ronald Reagan used human rights agenda and the bully pulpit at the same time, promoting rapprochement with Gorbachev because he could have rapprochement with Gorbachev. So, in very sensitive cases—you look at a Saudi Arabia or a Bahrain—what do you do? At the same time, you would—I can see a Magnitsky Act for Iran, easily, because that regime is involved in gross violations of human rights, day in and day out.

So, this is a foreign policy and national security matter, as well as a human rights matter. But, yes, the Magnitsky Act should be a blueprint and a model for America to stand for what we are.

Thank you.

Senator MCCAIN. Thank you.

Mr. Nemtsov, it is always a pleasure to see you.

Mr. NEMTSOV. Yes, thank you very much, Senator.

Senator MCCAIN. You not only inform, but you entertain. [Laughter.]

Mr. NEMTSOV. Well, first of all, I want to tell you that Magnitsky Act for Europe is absolutely crucial, even more important to come back to human rights and rule of law in Russia than American Magnitsky Act, because corrupted bureaucrats around Putin, they mainly spend vacations and send their kids to European universities, they have accounts, not in American, but Swiss, banks, they relax in the south of France, et cetera. That is why the response from Kremlin is terrible, as far as European opportunity for Magnitsky is concerned.

The last example of Irish Parliament discussion about Magnitsky Act was said—you know, that Russian Ambassador in Ireland sent a letter, to every deputies in Irish Parliament, that, "Guys, be careful. If you vote for Magnitsky in Ireland, we stop adoption." Stop adoption for kids, right? And a few hundred families—Irish families—press, deputies, and ask them, do not vote for that. It does not happen. Another opportunity is to use gas—I mean, Gazprom, et cetera—like a tool, to stop this Magnitsky. Well—but this is very important.

Second, I believe that Magnitsky Act is very, very pro-Russian law, because this is replacement of sanctions from the state—sanctions against the state to sanctions against corrupted and criminals, which is good. And Russian people, nevertheless what has happened on Putin TV, they understand that it is not against ordinary Russian people, this is against corrupted, murders, terrible guys.

And, last point, I believe that we will forget about Magnitsky Act when we come back to independent justice in Russia, because if we have independent court, why do you need some acts outside? If you are criminal, you will be in jail. That is it. But, this is not for Putin Russia.

Well, as far as list is concerned, I do not agree that this is like a symbolic. I do not think so. For example, there are some names, including friends of Putin, who are responsible for political repression, and our guys from an investigative committee, for example, or people who made the decision concerning Mikhail Khodorkovsky, right? Well, I think that, if such guys, we would be, in the least, not low profile guys, but serious guys—I think that this is not symbolic. This is a system. System based on corrupted person who are absolutely out of control. But, if they appear in this list, and the Europeans, for example, bomb the—them just—a visa, it will be the end of the story, believe me.

Senator McCAIN. I thank you.

Thank you, Mr. Chairman.

Senator MURPHY. Thank you, Senator McCain.

Mr. Sestanovich, I wanted to come back to this idea of the United States-Russian civil society fund. So, we are dealing with the ongoing persecution of NGOs. The Russians are acutely looking to see which of those we are funding. USAID has had to leave. How do you thread this needle? I mean, if we create a new fund that is funding NGOs, does not that essentially become a red, blinking light for Putin to watch for as he tries to figure out which NGOs to shut down? And, in this context, how do you do transparent, open support from the U.S. Government or from a civil society fund to NGOs, when that will just become a big advertisement for Putin as to who he should go after?

Ambassador SESTANOVICH. Senator, it is a good question. I am a member of the board of the National Endowment for Democracy, I should say, at the beginning. So, the favorable things I am going to say about NED's record should be heard with that in mind.

I think, even if you had not had this wave of repression in the past year in Russia, there are reasons to doubt the effectiveness of AID as a dispenser of assistance to civil society. It made it a government-to-government irritant. It involved an awful lot of bureaucratic overhead in Washington, a lot of inflexibility, slow moving. The National Endowment has a different track record and different mode, which is to operate with smaller grants, with a lot more flexibility, more rapid lead times, and has had an ability to support a lot of groups that would not have been able to benefit from AID's approaches.

The civil society fund that I mentioned could be administered by an organization like the NED. And I think you'd have some significant benefits in doing that.

Would the Russian Government dislike that reality? Yes. No question about it. But, the Russian Government is on weak ground, internationally, in trying to repress support for civil society. They are really isolated, in terms of international norms, and this is going to have to be an issue that we, and other like-minded countries, challenge them on. It is going to be a disagreement. We do not have to shy away from that.

Senator MURPHY. Mr. Nemtsov, we are going to all be watching the Navalny trial with great interest to see what it suggests about the lines that are going to be drawn, in terms of political prosecutions. I want to ask you a very simple question that you have answered privately, and ask you to answer it here.

Why are you not on trial today? And what does that say about the lines that are being drawn today, in terms of who is prosecuted and who is not? And is there any hope, in the fact that you are able to sit here today and testify in front of this committee and go back, later today, to Russia to continue your activities?

Mr. NEMTSOV. Well, this is the most popular question to me everywhere in the world, including America.

Well, I think that the best way is to ask this question to Putin, not to me, because he is responsible for jail, not me. Well, it is a first-second. I think that, when I was in jail, I want to tell you that it was huge response from the world, including the U.S. Senate, including Mr. McCain, including Mr. Cardin, including a lot of officials here and in Strasbourg, in Brussels. For Putin, it will be very difficult to explain that I am a criminal. It is very difficult. Of course, his investigative groups investigate—has already investigated all of my business before, and tried to find something. I am sure that if they will be successful, I'm not be here. Well, but they worked, hard, every day.

Well, next point, he is not Stalin. He is a combination of Stalin and Abramovich, oligarch, billionaire, to relax, to be recognized, et cetera. To organize absolutely clear political case—the case against me is 100 percent political. Everybody understand that. This is not even Khodorkovsky, because Khodorkovsky was the average guy, he took part in privatization, he took part in the shares-for-loans scheme, et cetera, et cetera. That is why, to explain, the world, that he is not because of politics, but he is because of no taxation, et cetera, it is easy. With me, to explain that I am the cause of taxation, is in jail, it is impossible, right?

Well, and he believes that criminal cases against Navalny is a sign to every opposition leaders to be quiet. To emigrate or to sit still. And he believe that if he will push Navalny, the rest will be relaxed and be great, to repeat the experience of Guriev and Kasparov——

Senator MURPHY. Right.

Mr. NEMTSOV [continuing]. And that's it.

Senator MURPHY. Right.

Mr. NEMTSOV. But, he is not right. I want to tell you that we will continue our fight.

Senator MURPHY. Good.

Senator Johnson and I have both done second rounds. Senator McCain, anything further?

Senator MCCAIN. No, I just want to thank all of the witnesses for their continued advocacy for democracy, not only in Russia, but especially in Russia. Your voices are well respected.

And, Mr. Jannuzi, I understand that you cannot take a position on some of these issues, but I also think that some of your public activities have been very helpful on behalf of the oppressed.

And, Boris, I am not quite as optimistic about—Boris, pay attention——

[Laughter.]

Mr. NEMTSOV. Excuse me. I explain what is happening. I have my flight at 3 o'clock. That is why I——

Senator McCain. All right. I just want to say I am not quite as optimistic about——

Mr. Nemtsov [continuing]. If I will be here, it will be great signal for Putin, you know. [Laughter.]

That is why the best way for me to leave now.

Senator McCain. I just want you to be careful, because I am not quite as optimistic as you are about Mr. Putin's desire to stifle opposition. So, you will be in our thoughts and our prayers as you continue your activities.

And I thank the other three witnesses. I read them all the time. It is nice to see you in person.

Thank you, Mr. Chairman.

Senator Murphy. Thank you, Senator McCain. We will get Mr. Nemtsov to his flights.

Thank you, to all five of you. As you have heard, we are very interested in following up with some communication to the President that we will work with you on.

Senator Murphy. And, with that, our hearing is adjourned.

[Whereupon, at 11:56 a.m., the hearing was adjourned.]

———

ADDITIONAL MATERIAL SUBMITTED FOR THE RECORD

Pussy Riot Collective Statement Submitted by Senator Barbara Boxer

Last week, members of our collective, Pussy Riot, visited Washington, DC, to meet with the U.S. State Department and Members of Congress who might help release two of our friends, Maria Alyokhina and Nadezhda Tolokonnikova, who are imprisoned in penal colonies in Russia, for the crime of hooliganism motivated by religious hatred.

They have been sentenced to 2 years in prison as extremists, receiving harsh punishments like vicious neo-Nazis and ultranationalists responsible for hate crimes against ethnic minorities, and are serving time alongside violent criminals, including murderers.

Our friends are mothers with small children. They are artists who are expressing our social and political views. Nothing more.

We are a collective of women active in feminist, LGBT, environmental, and other causes in Russia. We formed in advance of Vladimir Putin's return to the Presidency, which has been marred by deteriorating human rights conditions in Russia.

Our band stands for many freedoms, including our feminist values. These are values that directly contradict the culture of the ''macho man,'' led by Vladimir Putin that marginalizes women and degrades our role in society.

Many Russians did not pay attention to politics, but by 2011 they saw an arrogance in Putin, and it has activated people, many of whom have taken to the streets in protest. It activated us too. And for our protests, two of us were carted off to a penal colony, as violent criminals. The Russian Government is attempting to use all the institutions at its power—courts, the Duma, church—to suppress dissent.

We are but one example of dissenters who have been charged with crimes since Vladimir Putin's inauguration.

We urge the United States to take notice of what is happening in Russia, of how we are slipping backwards, not toward progress, but toward repression. We ask you, members of the Senate, to work for the release of our friends who aren't hooligans or criminals, but women who have strong views and the courage to voice them. Thank you.

———

MATERIAL SUBMITTED BY FRANK JANNUZI AS AN ATTACHMENT TO HIS PREPARED STATEMENT

APPENDIX: CHRONICLE OF RIGHTS VIOLATIONS IN RUSSIA

[Drawn from Amnesty International's 2013 Annual Report, available on-line here: *http://www.amnesty.org/en/region/russia/report-2013-page]*

Vladimir Putin's return as President, following widely criticized elections, led to a surge in popular protest and demands for greater civil and political freedoms, particularly around his inauguration in May. The result was increased restrictions. Protests were frequently banned and disrupted. New laws were adopted, often without public consultation and in the face of widespread criticism, which introduced harsh administrative and criminal penalties that could be used to target legitimate protest and political and civil society activities, and to restrict foreign funding for civic activism.

The Russian Federation responded belligerently to international criticism of its human rights record. A law on travel and other sanctions on officials allegedly responsible for the death of lawyer Sergei Magnitsky in custody in 2009 was passed by Congress and proposed in several other countries. The Russian authorities retaliated with reciprocal sanctions and by banning the adoption of Russian children by U.S. citizens and prohibiting Russian NGOs from receiving funding from the USA.

Freedom of assembly

Peaceful protests across Russia, including gatherings of small groups of people who presented no public threat or inconvenience, were routinely dispersed by police, often with excessive force. The authorities regarded every such event, however peaceful and insignificant in number, as unlawful unless expressly sanctioned, although gatherings of pro-government or pro-Orthodox Church activists were often allowed to proceed uninterrupted even without authorization. There were frequent reports of police brutality toward peaceful protesters and journalists, but these were not effectively investigated.

On 6 May 2012, the day before the inauguration of President Putin, a column of protesters moving along a permitted route to Bolotnaya Square in Moscow was halted by police, resulting in a standoff and localized skirmishes. Subsequently, 19 protesters faced criminal charges in connection with events characterized by authorities as "mass riots"; one pleaded guilty and was sentenced to 4½ years' imprisonment; the remainders were still awaiting trial at the end of the year. Several leading political activists were named as witnesses in the case and had their homes searched in operations that were widely broadcast by state-controlled television channels. Over 6 and 7 May, hundreds of peaceful individuals were arrested across Moscow, some merely for wearing white ribbons as a symbol of protest against electoral fraud.

The law governing public events was further amended in June. It expanded the list of violations, introduced new restrictions and increased sanctions.

Freedom of expression

The right to freedom of expression was increasingly restricted. Most media remained under effective state control, except for some outlets with limited circulation. Prime-time national television was regularly employed to smear government critics.

Libel was recriminalized, 8 months after its decriminalization. Changes to the Criminal Code expanded the definitions of treason and espionage and made them vaguer by including sharing information with, or providing miscellaneous assistance to, foreign states and organizations whose activity is "directed against security of the Russian Federation."

New legislation gave the government powers to blacklist and block Web sites publishing materials considered "extremist" or otherwise harmful to public health, morals, or safety. By the end of the year, this legislation was already being used to shut down sites publishing content protected by the right to freedom of expression.

Maria Alekhina, Ekaterina Samutsevich and Nadezhda Tolokonnikova, members of the punk group Pussy Riot, were arrested in March after a brief and peaceful, albeit provocative, political performance in the Cathedral of Christ the Saviour in Moscow. They were convicted of "hooliganism motivated by religious hatred" in August and were each sentenced to 2 years in prison, although Ekaterina Samutsevich received a conditional sentence on appeal and was released on 10 October. On 29 November a Moscow court declared video footage of the group's church performance "extremist," rendering its publication on the Internet unlawful.

Discrimination

Discrimination on grounds such as race, ethnicity, gender, religion, or political affiliation remained widespread. Discriminatory legislation targeting LGBTI individuals was introduced in several regions and proposed at the federal level. A law banning "propaganda of sodomy, lesbianism, bisexualism, and transgenderness among minors" came into force in St Petersburg in April. Similar laws were also introduced in Bashkiria, Chukotka, Krasnodar, Magadan, Novosibirsk, and Samara regions, and tabled before the State Duma. A number of public LGBTI events were forbidden and participants dispersed by police.

Across Russia, LGBTI individuals and members of various minority groups continued to face attacks. Such attacks were not effectively investigated by the authorities, and the perpetrators often remain unidentified.

On 4 August, four men forcibly entered an LGBTI club in Tyumen and physically and verbally assaulted several customers. Police detained the attackers. When the victims came to the police station to file complaints, they were left in the same room with the perpetrators, who continued to threaten them and were later released without charge.

Human rights defenders

Reports of harassment of human rights defenders continued. In the North Caucasus and elsewhere, activists, journalists and lawyers representing victims of human rights violations continued to face physical threats, including from law enforcement officials.

Investigations into many past attacks, including the killing of Natalia Estemirova, made no ostensible progress.

New legislation introduced further administrative hurdles and a legal obligation for NGOs to register as "organizations performing the functions of foreign agents" (language evocative of espionage) if they received foreign funding and engaged in broadly defined "political activities." Failure to comply with these provisions might lead to heavy fines, and imprisonment for NGO leaders.

Public officials routinely sought to blacken the reputation of individual human rights defenders and specific NGOs, as well as the work of human rights NGOs in general.

In October, a senior Federal Security Service (FSB) official reportedly stated that the FSB had secured the closure of 20 NGOs in Ingushetia for their links with foreign intelligence services. He provided no information either on any specific case involving charges of espionage against an NGO in Ingushetia, or on which NGOs had supposedly been closed for this reason. However, he singled out the well-known Ingushetian human rights NGO, Mashr, as a "foreign agent" still in operation.

On 20 January, lawyer Omar Saidmagomedov and his cousin were shot dead in Makhachkala, Dagestan, by security officials. The authorities reported the incident as a killing of two armed group members during a shoot-out. Omar Saidmagomedov's colleagues dismissed this report and demanded an investigation into allegations that he had been extra judicially executed because of his professional activities. The investigator summoned the lawyer representing Omar Saidmagomedov's family for questioning as a witness, apparently with the aim of disqualifying him from acting as legal counsel in the case.

Elena Milashina, a journalist from the independent newspaper Novaya Gazeta, together with a friend, was assaulted by two men in the street in Moscow on 4 April, and received serious injuries. The investigator identified and charged two individuals who initially signed confessions but retracted them after their families hired independent lawyers. The investigator ignored protests by Elena Milashina that the two did not fit her friend's description of the men who assaulted her and that the real perpetrators had not been identified.

Igor Kalyapin, head of the NGO Committee Against Torture, was threatened with criminal proceedings in connection with his work on the case of Islam Umarpashaev, torture victim from Chechnya. On 7 July, Igor Kalyapin was summoned by a criminal investigator for questioning for allegedly disseminating confidential information. In September, journalists who had interviewed Igor Kalyapin and individuals who wrote letters to show their support were summoned for questioning.

Torture and other ill-treatment

Allegations of torture and other ill-treatment remained widely reported and effective investigations were rare. Law enforcement officials allegedly frequently circumvented the existing legal safeguards against torture through, among other things: the use of secret detention (particularly in the North Caucasus); the use of force supposedly to restrain violent detainees; investigators denying access to a lawyer of one's choice and favoring specific state-appointed lawyers who were known to ignore signs of torture.

In March, one torture case in Kazan was widely reported in the media after a man died of internal injuries in hospital. He claimed that he had been raped with a bottle at the police station. Several police officers were arrested and charged with abuse of power, and two were later sentenced to 2½ years' imprisonment respectively. Many more allegations of torture by police in Kazan and elsewhere followed media reports of this case. In response to an NGO initiative, the Head of the Investigative Committee decreed to create special departments to investigate crimes committed by law enforcement officials. However, the initiative was undermined by the failure to provide these departments with adequate staff resources.

On the night of 19 January, Issa Khashagulgov, held in a pretrial detention center in Vladikavkaz, North Ossetia, was allegedly taken to an undisclosed location and beaten and threatened with further violence for refusing to cooperate with the investigation against him. Reportedly, between 6 and 8 February he was transferred from the detention center to a different location in North Ossetia for several hours each day when his lawyers tried to see him, and subjected to ill-treatment. Issa Khashagulgov, suspected of armed group membership, had earlier been repeatedly transferred between different detention facilities while his family and lawyers were denied information about his whereabouts, sometimes for several days. His complaints were not investigated.

Russian opposition activist Leonid Razvozzhayev went missing on 19 October in Kiev, Ukraine, outside the office of a partner organization to UNHCR, the U.N. refugee agency. On 22 October, the Investigative Committee in Moscow stated that he had voluntarily returned to the Russian Federation and handed himself in to the authorities. Leonid Razvozzhayev disavowed this statement via his lawyer, and alleged that he had been abducted and smuggled into the country, held at a secret location, ill-treated and forced to sign a statement implicating him and other political activists in plotting mass disturbances in Russia on foreign orders. The Russian authorities dismissed his allegations and refused to investigate them.

Justice system

The need for judicial reform was widely acknowledged, including by senior officials. However, no effective steps were taken toward ensuring the independence of the judiciary. Reports of unfair trials were numerous and widespread. A range of court decisions, including those concerning extremism and economic and drug-related crimes, were affected by political considerations, and a growing number of convictions appeared politically motivated, including those of the Pussy Riot members. Allegations were frequently made of collusion between judges, prosecutors, investigators and other law enforcement officials resulting in unfair criminal convictions or disproportionate administrative penalties.

Lawyers across the country complained of procedural violations undermining their clients' right to a fair trial. These included denial of access to clients, detention of individuals as criminal suspects without promptly informing their lawyers and families, appointment of state-paid lawyers as defense counsel who are known to raise no objections about procedural violations and the use of ill-treatment.

Lawyer Rustam Matsev complained that on 31 May a senior police official at a pre-trial detention center in Nalchik, Kabardino-Balkaria, demanded that he should "stop teaching his defendant to lie" and convince him to withdraw a complaint about abduction and ill-treatment by police. The officer allegedly told Rustam Matsev that lawyers "get blocked" in the same way as members of armed groups during their "elimination" in security operations. The authorities refused to investigate the lawyer's allegations.

On 27 October, dozens of protesters lined up 50m apart (a form of picketing which requires no prior authorization) in front of the central FSB headquarters in Moscow. Later, when several known political activists tried to leave, surrounded by reporters, they were detained by police. On 30 October and 4 December respectively, activists Alexey Navalny and Sergei Udaltsov were fined nearly US$1,000 each for organizing and participating in an unauthorized rally that violated public order. The judge hearing Alexey Navalny's case reportedly declined his defense lawyer's request to cross-examine the police officers who had detained him, and refused to admit video footage of the event as evidence.

North Caucasus

The region remained highly volatile. Human rights violations in the context of security operations remained widespread.

Armed groups continued to launch attacks against security forces, local officials and civilians. A double bomb attack on 3 May in Makhachkala, Dagestan, left 13 people dead (including 8 police officers), and over 80 emergency and rescue workers were injured. On 28 August, an influential Dagestani Muslim cleric, Sheikh Said Afandi, and his five visitors were killed by a woman suicide bomber. Other attacks by armed groups took place across the North Caucasus.

Some republics sought to develop nonrepressive responses to the threats posed by armed groups. Commissions for Adaptation were established in Dagestan and Ingushetia with the aim of encouraging the surrender and reintegration into society of former members of armed groups. The Dagestani authorities adopted a more tolerant attitude toward Salafi Muslims.

However, security operations continued to be conducted on a regular basis throughout the region. In the course of these, numerous human rights violations by law enforcement officials were reported, including enforced disappearances, unlawful detentions, torture and other ill-treatment, and extrajudicial executions.

The authorities systematically failed to conduct effective, impartial, and prompt investigations into human rights violations by law enforcement officials, or to identify those responsible and bring them to justice. In some cases, criminal proceedings were initiated, but for the most part, the ensuing investigation either failed to establish the perpetrators or confirm involvement of officials in the relevant incidents, or concluded that there had been no violation by law enforcement officials. Only exceptional cases led to the prosecution of police officials for abuse of authority in connection with torture and other ill-treatment. Not a single case of enforced disappearance or alleged extrajudicial execution was resolved, and no perpetrators from any other law enforcement agency were brought to justice.

> Rustam Aushev, a 23-year-old resident of Ingushetia, was last seen on 17 February at Mineralnye Vody railway station in the neighboring Stavropol region. The next day, his relative spoke to staff at the station. They reported seeing a young man being detained by plain-clothes men and driven away in a Gazelle minivan, which was also captured on CCTV. A security guard had reportedly spoken to the minivan's driver asking it to be parked in the designated area, and was shown an FSB official's ID. Rustam Aushev's family reported these details to the authorities and demanded an investigation, but his fate and whereabouts were unknown at the end of the year.

In Ingushetia, the first ever trial of two former police officials concluded in Karabulak. Some charges related to the secret detention and torture of Zelimkhan Chitigov although the officials faced other charges as well. The announcement of the verdict was postponed repeatedly for almost 3 months, and on 7 November the judge sentenced one defendant to 8 years' imprisonment, and fully acquitted the other, his former superior. Allegations of intimidation of victims and witnesses had persisted throughout the trial, during which both defendants remained at large. No other perpetrators were identified despite Zelimkhan Chitigov naming at least one other official by name and alleging that many others had been involved in the incessant bouts of torture during the 3 days he was kept in secret detention.

ADDITIONAL RESOURCES: REPORTS AVAILABLE FROM AMNESTY INTERNATIONAL'S INTERNATIONAL SECRETARIAT ON RUSSIAN HUMAN RIGHTS CONDITIONS

The Circle of Injustice: Secutiry Operations and Human Rights Violations in Ingushetia (2012)
[*http://www.amnestyusa.org/sites/default/files/3680*lingushetialcoverlcontents lweb.pdf]

In recent years, the Russian authorities have tried to extend and diversify their approach to threats posed by armed groups. This approach in Russia usually comes coupled with scant regard for the rule of law, and results in Human Rights Abuses that hinder the entire region's stability. Citizens in Ingushetia are the victims of extrajudicial executions, secret and incommunicado detentions and torture. Authorities fail to investigate allegations of torture, or the investigations are inadequate especially of complaints and accusations against security forces. Amnesty also documents the purposeful meandering of the legislative process to delay the development of justice.

Security forces in the North Caucasus partake in covert operations with masked and camouflaged men that bare no distinguishable markings. This tactic helps them to set the groundwork for the elaborate process of misleading investigators, refusing accountability, denying secret detentions, and deferring justice. No one has ever been held accountable by the Russian Government for enforced disappearances or extrajudicial executions in the North Caucasus.

Confronting the Circle of Injustice: Threats and Pressure Faced by Lawyers in the N. Caucuses (2013)
[http://www.amnesty.org/en/library/asset/EUR46/003/2013/en/6af890a1-d79f-487d-bd39-2af4020a5835/eur460032013en.pdf]

Human rights violations such as enforced disappearances, unlawful killings, torture and other ill-treatment committed by members of law enforcement agencies are regularly reported from the North Caucasus and almost never effectively investigated. These violations, and the Russian authorities' systematic failure to investigate them effectively, produces a circle of injustice and leads to further violations of fundamental human rights. This in many cases includes the inability for defendants to access or choose their own lawyer. Furthermore the lawyers that are chosen to represent the defendants are coming under increasing pressure and threats from the criminal justice system.

This intimidation fundamentally undermines the right to a fair trial, and in turn makes the lawyers themselves victims of human rights abuse. The atmosphere of intimidation and harassment creates a festering environment for the continued "success" of a repressive justice system. The Lawyers who choose to defend the rights of individuals accused of military or political crimes, routinely come across procedural and institutional obstructions which limit their ability to see and communicate with their clients. They are threatened by law enforcement officials and often receive no assistance from their respective bar associations.

Illustrative Cases

- Rustam Matsev: As a defense lawyer, Matsev has worked on a number of cases of individuals accused of membership in armed groups, many of whom claimed to have been tortured and mistreated by law enforcement officials. Prior to a cross-examination of one of his clients, the officer who would question his client asked Matsev why he had "taught his client to lie." He was then warned that "During security operations, while eliminating members of armed groups, we block lawyers as well. We will definitely meet again. When you walk, always look back because we are watching you and know everything that you do." Matsev believes this was a direct threat against him, but when he filed a complaint with the authorities, he was informed that the officer was joking, and Matsev must have misunderstood him.
- Omar Saidmagomedov: Saidmagomedov acted as defense counsel for several individuals accused of being members of armed groups, and alleged the use of torture and fabrication of evidence for use in criminal proceedings against his clients. On January 20, 2012, Saidmagomedov and his cousin were murdered by security officials in front of his cousin's house. A news broadcast the same night reported that the incident was a security operation in which two armed criminals were fleeing law enforcement officials who were shot as they tried to escape. Saidmagomedov's family and colleagues have been prevented from pursuing the case.
- Sapiyat Magomedova: A criminal lawyer known for her work on cases involving human rights violations allegedly committed by law enforcement agencies in Dagestan, Magomedova was beaten by police officers while trying to gain access to her clients. When she filed a complaint about the beating, the police opened a criminal investigation to prove that she, in fact, had beaten the police officers. Magomedova was repeatedly pressured to drop the charges. In 2011, both Magomedova's case against the police officers and the officers' case against her were closed. Magomedova plans to appeal the decision to close the criminal investigation of the assault by police officers.

Freedom Under Threat: Clampdown on Freedoms of Expression, Assembly and Association in Russia (2013)
[http://www.amnestyusa.org/sites/default/files/eur4601120130en.pdf]

Vladimir Putin was inaugurated as President of the Russian Federation in May 2012. His election in March fueled protests all over Russia. From December 2011 to December 2012 at least 5,100 protestors have been arrested in more than 220 protest gatherings.

His administration's response to the protest movement has been almost entirely repressive. Through administrative and legal changes he has severely curtailed the rights to freedom of expression, association, and assembly. The rights of political opponents, human rights organizations and activists, and all Russian citizens wishing to raise their voice in protest have been curtailed. These rights are explicitly guaranteed to the people by the Russian Constitution.

[AIUSA's interactive timeline on the above report is here: *http://www.amnestyusa. org/russia/*]

ADDITIONAL RESOURCES: AMNESTY INTERNATIONAL'S PRISONERS OF CONSCIENCE (POCS) AND OTHER INDIVIDUALS AT RISK IN RUSSIA

Mikhail Khodrokovskii and Platon Lebedev (Prisoners of Conscience)

AI believes that there is a significant political context to the arrest and prosecution of Mikhail Khodrokovskii and Platon Lebedev. They were arrested in July 2003 and charged with seven counts of fraud, tax evasion, and embezzlement and were accused of defrauding the state of over $1 billion. Both men denied the charges against them and maintained that the case was politically motivated, as did many domestic human rights groups. After a trial lasting almost 1 year in May 2005 a court found them guilty and sentenced them to 9 years in prison. On appeal, Khodorkovskii's sentence was reduced to 8 years.

AI is concerned about a number of fair trial violations, both publicly and in letters to the Russian Government.

Mikhail Khodorkovskii: Khodorkovskii was arrested in 2003 and has faced two trials: Tax evasion and fraud and embezzlement and money laundering. He was an outspoken activist against government corruption and was once considered a potential leader for the anti-Putin opposition party. The international community has spoken out in support of Khodorkovskii and many believe that his arrest was politically motivated. AI expresses concern about the timing of the charges against him, the reported harassment of his lawyers, and cited procedural violations that could have exonerated him. He is married and has four children.

Platon Lebedev: AI declared Russian businessman Platon Lebedev a prisoner of conscience after his convictions on money laundering were upheld by a Moscow court in 2011. Lebedev was a close associate of Khodorkovskii and the fourth-largest shareholder in Yukos oil. AI believes that his arrest was politically motivated. He has spent 9 years in jail on dubious charges. He is married and has four children.

LAWYERS IN THE N. CAUCUSES (INDIVIDUALS AT RISK)

Omar Saidmagomedov—Saidmagomedov was a defense lawyer for several individuals accused of being members of armed groups. Many of his clients stated they had been mistreated by authorities and were the victims of torture. On January 20, 2012, Saidmagomedov and his cousin were murdered by security officials in front of his cousin's house. That same night, the authorities claimed that he was killed in a security operation in which "two armed criminals shot at police officers during their escape." Saidmagomedov's family and colleagues have been blocked by the judicial process when attempting to pursue his case.

Rustam Matsev—As a defense lawyer from Nalchik, Kabardino-Balkaria, Matsev has worked on a number of cases for individuals accused of membership in armed groups, many of whom claimed to have been tortured. For this representation he has received personal and direct threats against himself and his clients. He was threatened prior to a cross-examination of one of his clients, when an officer who would question his client accused Matsev of teaching his client to lie. He was then told, "During security operations, while eliminating members of armed groups we block lawyers as well. We will definitely meet again. When you walk, always look back because we are watching you and know everything that you do." The officer also kept insisting that his client should confess to the crime he had been charged with. Matsev perceived the officer's words as a direct veiled threat against him and a warning that a criminal case against him may be fabricated. He later filed a complaint with the authorities but it was dismissed.

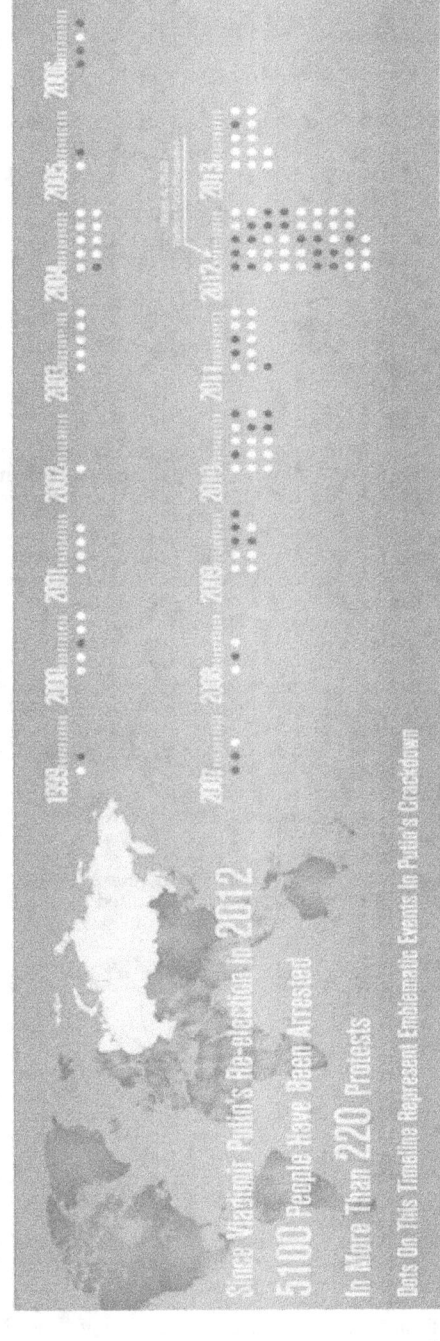

Two Articles Submitted for the Record by Leon Aron

[From the Washington Post, May 30, 2012]

Putin's War on Russian Civil Society Continues

(By Leon Aron, Published: Washington Post Opinions)

Almost a year into the Kremlin's war on civil society, the legal veneer looked familiar: A May 15 letter from prosecutors informed the Levada Center, Russia's most authoritative independent polling firm, that in publicizing the results of its polls it "aimed at shaping public opinion on government policy" and was, therefore, a "political organization." And, as a political organization receiving foreign grants (from the likes of the Ford and MacArthur foundations), it had to register as a "foreign agent."

Every assault on civil society is a tragedy for Russia. Nongovernmental organizations are, first and foremost, schools of democracy, teaching personal responsibility, self-organization, peaceful dissent and compromise. Left in their rubble are stagnation, hatred and radicalism. Yet even among the myriad instances of this state-directed civil catastrophe in the making, the (likely fatal) assault on the Levada Center stands out.

The last line of Pushkin's "Boris Godunov"—still a primer in Russian political tradition—is "Narod bezmolstvuet": "The people are silent." In a history strewn with tragedies and bad luck, it is hard to pinpoint the most damaging malady, but this silence is among the worst of Russia's ills. Of course, the people were never silent: They thought and they talked to one another, even if only in whispers. But all venues for influencing their country's course were severed—short of the periodic "bunt," or "Russian revolt, senseless and merciless" (Pushkin again). "We did not know the country in which we lived," Mikhail Gorbachev wrote in 1988.

So it was only natural that glasnost and public opinion polling in the Soviet Union were born in the same year: 1987. It was among the first and most exhilarating miracles of glasnost—a miracle of self-discovery: People learned what their fellow citizens thought! It was also among the surest signs that democratization was real. At long last, the country's leaders wanted to know people's views.

Leading the way was the All-Union Center for the Study of Public Opinion. Known by its Russian acronym, VTsIOM, the center was soon headed by the dean of Soviet sociologists, Yuri Alexandrovich Levada, who made it into the country's most respected polling firm.

But in September 2003 the Kremlin decided to "reclaim" VTsIOM, which was still nominally state-owned, and installed a new board of directors. The tipping point reportedly was tepid support for the four-year-old war in Chechnya. (The center publicized that 58 percent of Russians were against and only 27 percent for continuing it.) Levada quit—and the center's entire staff, more than 100 people, left with him. There was, however, still enough space unoccupied by the state for a new and independent polling firm, bearing Levada's name, to garner enough customers and supporters at home and abroad to sustain itself. Today, however, the government appears to have resolved to finish off the center.

For a regime that seems determined to deny the country desperately needed institutional reforms because they involve democratization—ensuring its short-term survival at the cost of the country's long-term stagnation—the letter was a logical move. All manner of findings routinely reported by the Levada Center in the past few months have flat-out contradicted the official propaganda narrative.

One in five Russians, the center found, were considering emigration, with the rate skyrocketing to 44 percent among 18- to 24-year-olds and 36 percent among those 25 to 39. A majority of Russians (57 percent) said that the Magnitsky Act—U.S. legislation that bars Russian officials involved in corruption and human rights abuses from entering the United States and from keeping money in U.S. banks—was aimed at those who "misuse power and violate human rights," or at the "meretricious and corrupt Russian bureaucracy," or at the country's leadership that covers up the misdeeds of "swindlers and embezzlers." By contrast, the government's assertion that the act was aimed "against Russia" was supported by only 23 percent. The final straw for the Kremlin may have been polling data on Putin's approval rating: It was at the lowest level in 12 years, Levada reported in January. Less than two weeks ago, the center found that if the presidential election were held this month, only 29 percent were ready to vote for Putin.

"We will continue our activity, although we are in a very difficult situation," Levada Center director Lev Gud kov, a man of a quick smile and impeccably objective analysis, recently told an interviewer. But it was "out of the question" for the center to register as a "foreign agent." "A totally new period has begun in Russia," he added, "the suppression of all independent organizations by the Kremlin."

Six and a half years ago in this newspaper, I said farewell to Yuri Levada, a great political sociologist and a dear friend. This news from Moscow is like burying him again.

————

[From the Wall Street Journal, June 10, 2013]

THE WIDENING PUTIN CLAMPDOWN

In today's Russia, even a moderate critic like Sergei Guriev is in danger of arrest.

(By Leon Aron)

In late May, Sergei Guriev, a prominent Russian economist and dean of Moscow's prestigious New Economic School, fled Russia fearing imminent arrest. His crime? Being critical of the Putin regime.

His concerns were well founded. Since February, Mr. Guriev had been interrogated more than once by Russia's Investigative Committee, the most feared of the Kremlin's tools of repression, and pressured to surrender personal and professional documents. He and his wife were under surveillance, his office searched, and five years of emails seized. He was told that his home would soon be searched.

Mr. Guriev was no opposition activist, much less an opposition leader—the typical targets of Kremlin harassment. To the contrary, while his incisive analytical articles (a must-read for all Russia watchers) were often critical of government policies—and while he never shied away from advocating the rule of law or condemning corruption—he was in many ways a consummate insider. A longtime adviser to the Kremlin, Mr. Guriev sat on the Presidential Commission on Open Government as well as the board of several state-run companies. Even after fleeing the country, he was re-elected to the board of Sberbank, SBRCY -2.90% Russia's state-controlled banking giant.

It is precisely Mr. Guriev's within-the-system position that makes the regime's attack on him so portentous and troubling. In forcing him into exile, the Kremlin has signaled a unilateral renegotiation of the long-standing social compact with liberal public-opinion leaders.

Not long ago, pro-reform members of the establishment could say and write what they pleased so long as they did not actively support the opposition. Now the message is: You must stop public criticism of the government—or risk harassment and even jail. If you don't like the deal, leave while the going is still good. Those who choose to stay, according to the popular opposition blogger Yulia Latynina, must "believe that the greatness of Russia lies in Vladimir Putin," and that criticism of him is part of a "world conspiracy" or "fifth column" machinations inside the Russian government.

Thus, a year into the authoritarian consolidation that followed Mr. Putin's re-election as president in March 2012, his government has entered a new phase of repression. The Guriev exile marks the beginning of the regime's transition from the softer authoritarianism of who is not against us is with us to a much harder and malignant version of who is not with us is against us.

This is on display in the continuing trial of popular opposition leader Alexei Navalny, a lawyer and anticorruption crusader who had the temerity to declare that he would challenge Mr. Putin in the 2018 election. Facing the unlikely charge that he stole 10,000 cubic meters of timber from a state-owned company while he was an unpaid adviser to a regional governor, Mr. Navalny faces a maximum sentence of 10 years.

Another opposition leader, Sergei Udaltsov of the Left Front movement, is awaiting trial under house arrest for his role in protests against Mr. Putin after last year's election. Mr. Udalstov is charged with the "preparation of riots and mass disorder," arranged with the help of the "government of Georgia." There is little doubt now that, like Mr. Navalny, he is likely to be sentenced "to the full spool of thread," as Russians say of a maximum sentence.

The Guriev ordeal also leaves little doubt about the fate of Russia's most famous prisoner, Mikhail Khodorkovsky, who more than a decade ago refused to heed Mr. Putin's warning to "stay out of politics." After two trials, two convictions and 10 years in jail, the former "oligarch" and principal owner of the now bankrupt oil giant Yukos is up for release next year. It would not be a surprise if the government found a reason to keep him in jail.

Mr. Guriev's key sin appears to have been his participation, with eight other law and economics experts, in a commission convoked in 2011, at then-President Dmitry Medvedev's request, to address a widespread revulsion over the second trial and conviction of Mr. Khodorkovsky and his business partner Platon Lebedev the previous year. Predictably, the independent commission found the state's case bogus.

In the regime's new mode of repression, the survival of Russia's few remaining independent media outlets looks precarious. These include Ekho Moskvy radio station, the Dozhd television and online station, and the Vedomosti daily and Novaya Gazeta twice-weekly newspapers. The main financier of the latter newspaper, former billionaire Alexander Lebedev, is on trial for ''malicious hooliganism'' for getting into a fist fight on live television. ''The full spool of thread'' for him would be five years. LiveJournal.com, where most opposition leaders blog, has in recent years been the target of several mysterious cyber attacks, causing it to shut down for short periods.

''It seems that Russia is entering a new period—the establishment of a dictatorship,'' a leading Russian political sociologist wrote to me in recent days. Earlier this spring, I would have asked if I could cite him by name and almost certainly would have received his permission. Now that even Sergei Guriev has fled the country, such a request was no longer safe to make without putting my correspondent in danger.

www.ingramcontent.com/pod-product-compliance
Lightning Source LLC
Chambersburg PA
CBHW080553290526
45790CB00006B/2639